The Conscious Entrepreneur's Guide to Creating Wealth

Michael Mapes

Michael Mapes
1744 West Catalpa St
Apt D10
Springfield, MO 65807
www.michaelmapes.org

Book Layout ©2014 BookDesignTemplates.com

Ordering Information:
Quantity sales. Special discounts are available on quantity purchases by corporations, associations, and others. For details, contact the "Special Sales Department" at the address above.

The Conscious Entrepreneur's Guide to
Creating Wealth/ Michael Mapes. —1st ed.

ISBN 13: 978-1508846406

Contents

Introduction 1

Chapter One: Why Wealth? Why Now? 7

Chapter Two: Laying the Foundation for a Truly
               Wealthy Business 31

Chapter Three: The Wealthy Entrepreneur 55

Chapter Four: The Power of Right Action 93

Chapter Five: How to Magnetize Yourself to Clients,
               Money and Opportunity 119

Chapter Six: Constructing Your Ultimate Client-Getting Plan.... 137

Chapter Seven: Writing Your New Wealth Story 159

Chapter Eight: The Three Essential Investments of a
               Wildly Successful Business Venture 191

Chapter Nine: Your Wealthy Future 227

About The Author 231

To my aunt Joi who taught me how to have a song in my heart even through the darkest of circumstances. And to my grandfather Arlo who showed me that sometimes you have to be stubborn when it comes to getting what you want. You may have left this world, but your presence, support, and kindness are with me always.

Love, Michael.

Introduction

When I first sat down to write a book about how to create more wealth in your life and in your business it was a surreal experience. For a child who had grown up in a trailer, raised by a single mother, who wore clothes from Goodwill, and entered adulthood with my self-esteem shattered and in a huge amount of emotional pain, to be writing a guide for entrepreneurs to make a lot of money while fulfilling their purpose and helping a lot of people seemed improbable at best and comical at worst. When I considered the power of the message I had to share, and the very real, very profound impact I know this information has on the lived experience of entrepreneurs, I realized not writing this book was simply unacceptable.

The information contained in this volume has transformed my life in ways that I could never have conceived of even just a few years ago. It has helped me create a six-figure business where I get to work with some amazing people, as well as an amazing team. It has helped me create a lifestyle that I adore living. It has allowed me to travel the world connecting with some amazing entrepreneurs who are truly changing the way we think, live and do business in the world. Most importantly, it has given me the knowledge each morning when I wake up that I am absolutely doing what I came to this planet to do.

My journey begins in a small town in northwest Iowa where I was born to very young parents. From the very beginning, I was outside the small town box, telling my preschool teacher at age five that I was psychic. You can imagine how thrilled she must have been to hear that information. My father left the same year, and it quickly became my sister, my mother, and later my brother, and myself against the world. A mentality I have alternately had to embrace, and let go of, to achieve the level of success I have.

Many of my first memories revolve around how hard my mother worked to provide for us, including often working two jobs while putting herself through school, where she would ultimately earn a PhD. I was smaller and more feminine than most of the other boys in my class, and by the time I was 12 being bullied and tormented was a daily occurrence. The love that I experienced within my family was my saving grace. It was the love and unconditional acceptance that I found there that instilled in me a deep knowledge of my own ability and potential. It would be many years before I fully connected with how to actualize this potential into a force that could actually improve my life, and subsequently the lives of others.

By the time I entered college, my self-esteem was virtually non-existent, and I was in an incredible amount of emotional pain. Despite being smart, I was an average student, often missing classes, and generally not taking my education seriously. The college experience, while really valuable in teaching me how to think about things, was not something that I was well suited for. I found most of my classes boring and uninteresting. I was much more interested in starting projects, and being a part of collaborations where I could get my hands dirty and see quick and immediate results. At the time, I thought this was because I was lazy and unfocused. I now realize it was because I was incredibly entrepreneurial.

After five years, I finally managed to graduate college at the height of the economic recession, when my already fragile reality collapsed. I had no job, the business I had started a few years before doing intuitive readings was providing nowhere near enough income to be able to pay my bills, and student loans were going to come due. I felt lost, depressed, and it felt like I was floating through life. I moved back into my mom's basement, and after a few months managed to land a job at a telemarketing firm where I was paid $8/hour.

The worst part of the entire experience was knowing in my heart that I had the potential to help a lot of people, and that I wasn't fulfilling that mission. I felt like a complete failure, and it finally dawned on me that I had to do something different. One day, I woke up and decided that I could no longer work at a job I hated, and so I packed my things, called a taxi cab, and begged a friend to let me stay on his couch in a nearby city. My family was shocked, but I knew I had to do something drastic to change my life.

Even though I was terrified, I remember hearing a deep voice within me that said, "Just take the next step." I listened. I committed in that moment to doing whatever it would take to live my life on my own terms, grow my business in a way that felt authentic, and make the impact that I knew I was meant to make. What I learned next forms the basis of this book.

Perhaps you've had your own "taxi cab" moment. That moment where staying right where you are seems like the most dangerous thing you could choose. Maybe you're stuck, struggling, or frustrated with the way your own life, or your own business, is going. Or maybe you've achieved success but you've done so in a way that requires you to sacrifice your own time or value system. Whatever position you're currently in, if you've picked up this book, one thing is certain: there's something within you that knows you are meant to do something important in the world.

Whether you want to deeply impact the lives of just a few people, or whether you see yourself serving the masses, if you've been led to this book, it's because there's something contained within that is going to help you achieve that mission. Even if you don't know it yet, there's something within you that desires to create more authentic wealth. I'm pulling back the curtain on what worked for me, and what I wish I would have known when I began this journey, and I genuinely believe that if you are really ready to experience miracles in your life, it will work for you as well.

I am not writing this book despite my circumstances, I am writing this book *because* of my circumstances. Each individual experience, including the ones that presented themselves as obstacles, hardships, or adversities, was actually a perfectly crafted lesson plan that gave me the skills, inner fortitude, and knowledge I needed to serve others in the way that is the most true for me. Every situation and circumstance you've lived through, all of the joys and all of the pains, can do the same for you, if you're open to this new way of interpreting your life and your reality.

If you're up for the journey, I don't promise it will be easy, pleasant or without challenge, but I do promise that it will show you a path to creating more wealth in every area of your life. Here's to changing your reality!

From my mind to yours,

Michael T. Mapes

CHAPTER ONE

Why Wealth? Why Now?

Most people don't really want to be wealthy. Yes! You read that right. Most people *don't* really want to be wealthy. Sure, when you ask them they'll say "Are you feeling OK?! Of course I want to make more money!"

Notice I didn't say that people won't tell you they want to be wealthy. I said:

Most people don't really want to be wealthy.

Wealth is about a lot more than just money, and we'll get there in a moment. For now, let me explain what I mean before you close this book and leave me a nasty Amazon review!

Have you ever had any of the following thoughts?

- *Making a lot of money only comes from years of hard work*

- *I'll never get ahead because good people finish last*

- *Rich people are greedy*

- *Earning a great income requires you to sacrifice your time and freedom*

- *You can't do something you love and make great money*

- *People who make money do so at the expense of others*

- *There's something unspiritual about making great money*

- *When you're wealthy people want to take it from you or they want something you have*

- *Having money requires selling out your values*

- *The IRS would come after you if you were rich*

- *The wealthy only give to charity for the tax breaks*

- *If I was rich I wouldn't know who my real friends are anymore*

- *I wouldn't be responsible if I had unlimited funds*

Have you ever been uncomfortable when one of your friends mentioned how much money they make at their job?

Or not expressed how much you make because you fear that someone else will judge you?

Have you ever resented your co-worker, family member, friend, and acquaintance or fellow entrepreneur because you know they make more than you?

What have you consciously done in the last 30 days to be able to create more income?

Starting to see the point?

We have a series of beliefs, conscious and unconscious, that make a lot of us pretty uncomfortable with the idea of being wealthy. Most of us have developed a dysfunctional relationship to money, wealth and in turn our own happiness. The, "Yes! I want to be wealthy!" thought occupies our brain for about half a millisecond before all of the fears, limiting beliefs, and self-sabotaging attitudes take over and prevent it from *ever becoming our reality.*

Maybe some of you are having a minor melt down right now. Arguing, resisting and loudly declaring, "No! That's not me. I really, really want to be wealthy!" And I don't doubt your integrity at all. You may really *want* it. Unfortunately, there's a difference between desiring something (even strongly), and actually creating the circumstances that will allow it to become reality. There's also a difference between desiring something and actually being in an energetic space to be able to see it made manifest in your life.

This is a get-your-hands-dirty kind of book, so let's not waste one more minute on your journey to becoming wealthier. Your first step to creating wealth as an entrepreneur starts right now.

You can tell how ready you are to create wealth by how strongly you embrace or resist my first wealth principle.

Wealth Alignment Principle: Authentic wealth begins by uncovering what negative conscious and unconscious beliefs you have around wealth, money, and success.

In short, admit you have a problem! Not the most original principle in the world granted, but relevant nonetheless. Whether healing our addiction to drugs and alcohol or negative money stories we begin in the same place. Admitting we have a problem, and understanding we can't fix it on our own.

Negative beliefs around money, wealth and success are very real forces that shape our ability to actually be able to create these things. Put another way, the thoughts we think have everything to do with the way we experience our world. Which means, if you want to create wealth in your life, you begin by changing your mind. Take a deep breath. Get ready to tell yourself the truth.

Write out all of the negative beliefs, attitudes, and stories you have about money.

_____

_____

_____

_____

_____

_____

_____

_____

_____

_____

_____

_____

_____

Were you honest with yourself? How aware were you that you were harboring these beliefs? Sorry! There are no points for being aware of them. Awareness begins our journey, but too many self-help books bring awareness to problems without providing the wisdom necessary for you to do anything about it. The result? You feel really bad about yourself, and not much happens in the way of transformation. This is not that kind of book. This is a book that will help you heal your relationship to wealth, to money, and to success so that you can show up in the world as the person, and the entrepreneur you were born to be.

Do you feel the urge right now to resist, hide, and ignore these beliefs? Good! That means we're touching something in desperate need of transformation. I'm not interested in getting angry at these beliefs, resenting them, and I'm not going to tell you that you need to get rid of them. Instead, by the end of this book, I'll show you how each of these "negative" beliefs actually hold beautiful, amazing wisdom. In order to glean that wisdom, and in order for you to live a wealthier life, we have to transform these beliefs, not belittle them.

For now, while we're on the topic of what kind of book this is and isn't:

What This Book Is Not

This book is not a step-by-step manual to building a business, although many of you will find gems of wisdom within these teachings that will enable you to take your businesses to new levels.

Don't worry. I'll give you some resources throughout the book for those of you that need this knowledge as well. I am absolutely committed to you getting the practical knowledge as well as the energetic shifts necessary to become successful. And believe me, I know what it takes to go from struggling to successful.

This book is not a magic solution to all of your problems, although if you engage critically with the concepts presented to you many of your problems will simply drift away as if by magic.

This book is not only for entrepreneurs, although I am an entrepreneur, and many of the teachings will have a deep resonance with entrepreneurs. If you are not an entrepreneur, and the teachings resonate with you, take them, use them, and share them.

This book is not a collection of action steps, although you will find many actions that you can take should they feel authentic and meaningful to you.

This book is not about teaching you anything, it's about allowing you to move past all of the barriers and blockages that have been in the way of YOU just being you. After all, YOU hold all the keys to wealth.

This book does not claim to help you make millions of dollars, mostly because why impose any limit at all on what you are capable of creating/earning?

This book is not a get rich quick book, although the principles contained within can absolutely make you rich.

This book is not the only way to become wealthy, or successful, or profitable in your business. It is *one way* to do those things.

This book is not solely about money, although many of you that read this will find new and creative ways to create more money than you've ever had in your lives.

This book will not tell you it's ok to meditate and visualize while never taking action, although the spiritual practices contained within are critical to being able to take inspired action that gets results. *Inspired action* is the bridge to your vision.

This book will not tell you it's OK to neglect doing your inner work or taking action because you're too tired, too busy, you have too many obligations, your partner won't like it, you don't have the money, or you're unsure of yourself. This is a book that will tell you, "Yes, that's true. Do it anyway."

This book will not tell you that you never have to make an investment or go outside of your comfort zone, although it will give you strategies and tools to be able to do those things consciously.

Why You Bought this Book

Now that that's out of the way, let's talk about why you bought this book. There is nothing contained in this manuscript that you don't already know. There are only things you have either forgotten or of which you aren't currently aware.

If you're reading this it's because there is a calling within your soul to live a much wealthier life. Sure there may have been a conscious reason why you chose to buy this book. Maybe you follow my work and like what I have to say. Maybe you were drawn to the promise of more money or financial freedom. Maybe you enjoy the self-help genre and were looking for another spiritual or manifesting technique to *finally* allow you to step into abundance. Maybe you just liked the cover. Or maybe you've been struggling or feeling unfulfilled in your business and you're looking for a way out.

The truth is if you're still reading it's because something greater brought you here. Why? Because you are ready to live your life and run your business in a way that works for your good, the good of your clients, and the good of the world.

This book will help you make more money, grow your business, and give you some of the most powerful techniques I know to strengthen your ability to consciously and creatively create wealth in your life and in your business. It will give you the inner tools that you need to be able to take the external action, and it will enable you to become the ultimate designer of your life.

The Conscious Entrepreneur

Before we go any further, I want to clarify what I mean when I use the term conscious entrepreneur. There are so many different terms out there to describe the new generation entrepreneurs that are starting businesses that make great money, while also reflecting a new, more progressive set of values. Spiritual entrepreneurs, holistic entrepreneurs, heart-centered entrepreneurs, transformational entrepreneurs, are just a few of the words used to describe this new generation of entrepreneurs. While these words do a decent job of categorizing these entrepreneurs, they all come with their limitations.

A conscious entrepreneur is an entrepreneur who makes great money, and creates a big impact by helping a lot of people, while living a life they love and doing so in a way that is ethical, authentic, and meaningful. Conscious entrepreneurs bring a higher level of awareness to every element of their business, from the values they instill in their team, to the level of service they provide their customers, to listening to their intuition when they make daily decisions, to the vendors they choose to work with, and of course to the actual work they deliver or products they sell.

Conscious entrepreneurs are in every industry. Just because someone is in a helping or healing profession, doesn't necessarily mean they are conscious. I've seen several so-called spiritual entrepreneurs who bring a very low level of awareness to their work, and several so-called "traditional" business owners who are completely transforming the world by the way they run their businesses and the way they choose to live their lives, and vice versa.

It's not a stretch to say the old way of doing business hasn't worked. It's resulted in a huge majority of our population being dissatisfied with their work, contributed to global conflict, poverty and strife, and resulted in an economic slow-down that has proved disastrous to millions. Conscious entrepreneurs understand that environmental protection, gender equality, fair labor practices, employee satisfaction, and a host of other social issues are not incompatible values with business growth and profit. In fact, creating new businesses that contribute to and enhance our planet is the only way forward if we want to continue to survive, and ultimately thrive, as a species.

Whether business continues to evolve into a force for social good or whether we continue to build businesses that reflect an outdated value system is the crossroad we now find ourselves at.

I believe that conscious entrepreneurs hold the key to a positive evolution of business, wealth, money, and success. For every conscious entrepreneur that achieves true success, we demonstrate that it is possible to build businesses in a way that is ethical and betters, rather than destroys, our planet.

Money vs. Wealth

The use of the word wealth, and the decision to write a book about how you can be wealthy, is a very conscious decision. I had initially intended to write a book laying out the step-by-step formula that you could use to create a business, when the idea flooded into my brain directly from Spirit that what entrepreneurs need right now is not just another guide about how to get clients and make money, but a comprehensive system to be able to reconfigure their spiritual DNA so that attracting wealth and success becomes easy and natural.

There are millionaires who have no idea what it means to be wealthy. Wealth is not simply about making great money. Wealth is a feeling, a mindset, as well as an external experience. I define wealth as being able to live your life in whatever way is most authentic to you without worry. Wealth is a holistic way of looking at the human experience.

My spiritual mentor Lynda Austin once said to me, "We all have abundance. The question is of what do you have an abundance?" Meaning do you have an abundance of money, of friends, of happiness, or do you have an abundance of sadness, of victimhood, of excuses or of lack?

Money plays a part in this equation, but there's no universal magic amount of money that contributes to feeling wealthy. For me, wealth is about having a wealth of friends and family support, it's about having a wealth of financial resources, and it's about having a wealth of kindness and generosity in my heart as much as possible.

We are not copies of one another. The amount of money I need to feel wealthy may be very different from the amount you need to feel wealthy. Neither of us are right or wrong. Money is simply energy. How much of that energy you desire to create or attract into your life is entirely up to you.

Wealth Alignment Principle: Feeling wealthy is a precursor to being wealthy.

The decision to feel wealthy is not out of your control. It has nothing to do with how much money is currently in your bank account. It has nothing to do with whether or not you feel supported. It has nothing to do with where you live, what kind of car you drive, or what clothes you wear. Feeling wealthy is a choice that you can make no matter what circumstances you see presently reflected around you.

In order to feel wealthy, you must have some sense of what your life would look like when you actually achieve it. Have you ever actually taken the time to consider what genuine wealth looks like for you? How can you possibly hope to attract it without considering what it might actually entail? I'm going to walk you through an exercise that will help you gain clarity around what wealth means (and looks like) to you.

As you go through this exercise, release the need to judge yourself or compare yourself to others. The answers to the following questions are contained within you, and answering honestly and in integrity is essential.

What does authentic wealth look like for you?

_____

_____

_____

_____

_____

_____

_____

_____

_____

_____

_____

_____

_____

How would your life be different if you truly felt wealthy?

_____

_____

_____

_____

_____

_____

_____

_____

_____

_____

For the next seven days, every morning, read what you've written. Spend just a few minutes to connect deeply with the feeling of wealth. Visualize yourself living your perfect wealthy life, and allow your walls to fall and the feeling of wealth to become normal.

You may resist this at first. That's OK! Remind yourself that you are so much more than worthy of living this wealthy, happy, fulfilled life. Move through your barriers and inner blockages, and begin to receive this visualization, this possibility at a more profound level.

True wealth also has nothing to do with being greedy. Greed is a decision that someone makes, it actually has nothing to do with how much money someone has. Greed is choosing to withhold from others out of fear that there isn't enough to go around. We can be greedy with our money, just as we can be greedy with our emotions. Have you ever withheld love from someone out of fear? What about forgiveness? Have you avoided giving to a charity you believed deeply in out of fear? Greed is a choice, not a reflection of how much someone has or doesn't have.

A client once told me that she desperately wanted to add another bathroom, but was uncomfortable doing so because some people in the world didn't have a bathroom at all. As if her getting an additional bathroom had anything to do with whether or not someone else did. Have you bought into the lie that there are a limited number of resources, and that you getting something takes away from someone else's ability to get something?

Wealth Alignment Principle: There is an unlimited amount of wealth. Being wealthy doesn't take anything away from anyone, it actually grants the ability to give back in much bigger ways.

Let's take my client for example. How different would her life have been if she saw herself as resourceful enough to re-do her bathroom? Perhaps she would have shown up less stressed every single day because she would have eliminated the crazy rush her family experienced each morning. Perhaps she would have discovered that she had the power to create the resources necessary to make positive changes in her life, and shared that message with others.

The point is not whether someone gets a new bathroom. The point is that when we step into abundance we show up in the world in a more positive way, and we enable and encourage others to do the same. My client's reaction only makes sense if you believe we live in a limited and finite world.

I believe we have all of the resources we need to for every single person on the planet to live a happy, healthy, and YES even a wealthy life. Acceptance of this deep truth creates wealth. Rejection of this deep truth repels wealth and fosters guilt and bitterness.

When we allow ourselves to become wealthy, we actually have more to give to others. On the surface level, we have more money to give to the causes and charities we care about. On a deeper level, when we allow ourselves to receive wealth, we have more energy, more love, more time, and more compassion. Greed comes from fear, wealth comes from love.

An Orientation in Comfort

I've got some bad news! Wealth, success in business, and lasting happiness is not created from a place that makes you feel comfortable. Anytime my Elite or Visionary Elite Clients (my high-end clients) are unsure about what step to take next, we look at what action would make them uncomfortable. Usually in examining this we are able to chart the next inspired action to take. Which brings us to our next Wealth Alignment Principle.

Wealth Alignment Principle: True wealth is created by an ongoing willingness to be uncomfortable.

From the time we are children we are taught to protect ourselves, to keep our true selves hidden, and to prioritize feeling pleasant above all else. I was lucky enough to have a mother with an incredibly strong sense of justice, so I received a counter message to the oppressive cultural teaching of comfort at all cost. My mother taught me that doing the right thing was more important than doing the easy thing.

The result of this was that I learned to prioritize my goals, my values, and taking right action over doing things simply because they didn't rock the boat. How does this relate to building your business and creating wealth? For most of us, myself included, we were not taught how to have a prosperous and abundant relationship to money. Instead we were taught that money was scarce, something to be carefully spent, or horded.

If you want to unlearn these lessons, which penetrate very deep into your subconscious, and replace them with the lessons of wealth, it's going to be uncomfortable. You're going to have to challenge your assumptions about money, about how you make decisions and about where to invest your resources. You're going to have people tell you you're crazy, that your dreams will never become reality, and that you should just go get a job like everyone else. You have to be willing to ask people for more money than you've ever been paid before. You have to be willing to handle and deal with rejection in a way that propels you forward instead of stagnates you.

None of these things are going to feel great all the time. The silver lining? If you are willing to get comfortable being uncomfortable you will come out a stronger, more prosperous person, and the wall between thought and form will begin to crumble. The moment you have an idea that you want to see become real, you will begin to be able to create it.

There's no time like the present to start our journey of feeling uncomfortable and resistant. I want you to make a list of 3 actions that you *know* would help you grow your business that you have been avoiding because they make you feel afraid or uncomfortable. If you don't get mildly sick looking at your list, start over, you've lied to yourself and written down comfortable actions.

1. _____

2. _____

3. _____

Here is where a lot of people stop. Or they try to just force themselves to take the action. But the answer to moving through discomfort and taking action does not lie in willpower. I'm going to share with you the process I use with clients to allow them to heal their limitations at deep levels and take the actions that will *actually* move them toward their vision.

One note before I share this powerful healing technique with you. You do not need to remove all traces of discomfort. You only need to be able to clear enough discomfort to be able to take the action that will move you to where you want to be.

Look over your list. Next to each action item I want you to write down what the deeper fear is behind taking the action. For example, maybe you wrote down "Make a sales call to a potential client." Is the fear that they'll reject you? Is the fear that the call will be uninvited? Is the fear that they will think something negative about you? Is the fear that you won't say the right thing?

After you've identified what the *real* fear is, I want you to consider from where this fear originated. Did you hear negative things about sales people growing up? Were you told to be quiet and not to bother the adults? Maybe you were told that you always put your foot in your mouth, and you need to be more polite.

Are you beginning to see how your resistance to taking these actions isn't coming from the present version of yourself? It's coming from a previous, often childhood version of yourself!

How different would you feel about taking these actions if the adult you got into the driver seat, and took the action?

Now that you understand these fears are coming from an older version of yourself, I want you to figure out what you need to tell this older version of yourself to be able to take the action. Think, "What would this older version of myself need to be told so that I can feel safe enough to take action that is in my best interest?"

Perhaps this version of yourself needs to be told that you will handle any rejection or fear, and they can simply relax and know they are safe. Maybe this part of yourself needs to be told it is loved and perfect, and no external reaction can change that reality.

What is it these versions of yourself need to hear in order for you to take action that will create wealth?

_____

_____

_____

_____

_____

_____

_____

_____

_____

_____

_____

_____

What most people do is judge, resent, and criticize these parts of themselves, which breeds more fear and inaction. Inaction is merely the natural reaction to an unhealed wound. Imagine breaking your arm, and instead of going to the doctor, having it fitted for a cast, and creating space to heal – you simply went through your daily life as if nothing was wrong. How long could you keep going before you completely broke down?

Yet that is exactly what you're doing in your business. Ignoring old wounds instead of healing them. Is it really any wonder you aren't getting the results you want? I invite you to walk yourself through this healing process any time you find yourself unable or unwilling to take the action that will move your business, and your quest for wealth forward.

Go back to your list of action steps. How do you feel about taking these actions now? Hopefully you feel noticeably more comfortable and confident. If not, spend some time in meditation speaking to the wounded versions of yourself letting them know they are loved, supported, and accepted.

Make a commitment to yourself, *right now*, to take action on *at least* one of these action items. After you take action, celebrate yourself, and know that you've just taken a huge step forward.

What to Expect Moving Forward

This book is not about a simple "step-by-step" formula. Anyone who tells you that you can simply follow a set of steps and be successful is being completely disingenuous. While there are steps you can take, success has as much to do with doing your inner work as it does following a series of steps. Part of becoming successful is defining and understanding what success looks like for you. How could someone else develop a set of action steps that would lead you to your ultimate success?

Instead, I aim to create a sacred experience for you, that will allow you to become a person for whom success and wealth flows easily and authentically. This person is already within you. All this book will do is allow him or her to emerge.

Now our final Wealth Alignment Principle of this Chapter.

Wealth Alignment Principle: Successful people understand that life is a constant state of expansion and contraction. They don't expect every day to go according to their plan, they expect that there is a grander plan – and their job is to show up every day and play their part in it.

There's a certainty that your journey to success will be uncertain. It will not go according to your plan, and it will require you to stretch, to grow, and to acknowledge some hard things about the choices you've made. It will also be filled with amazing breakthroughs, huge joys, and you'll discover that you are capable of things you never imagined.

Are you willing to take this journey with me? Are you willing to begin to see every circumstance or experience in your life, good or bad, as offering you something that you can use to serve others, and will help you grow? If not, no worries! There's absolutely nothing wrong with wanting to stay right where you are, if it's completely authentic to you.

But if you feel you were destined for something more. If this Chapter has resonated with you on a deeper level than anything you've read in a while, and if you are serious about creating and attracting more wealth into your life and into your business, then read on.

CHAPTER TWO

Laying the Foundation for a Truly Wealthy Business

L et me be honest with you. I did basically everything "wrong" when it came to starting and then running my business. I paid no attention to the order in which things were "supposed" to be done. I had zero business, marketing, administrative, or sale training. I didn't even know a single business owner or entrepreneur. What I did have was a desire to help people and a big drive to be successful.

I learned so much through the experiences of doing everything backwards, sideways, and out-of-order, because I learned what works, what doesn't work, when to do things, and when not to do things. I wouldn't want anyone to have to go through everything that I went through to become successful. There was no reason I had to go through it either, except that I simply didn't know there was another way.

The hardest part of all of this was going through a period where I felt like I wasn't living my purpose, because the success of my business was not matching up to the drive I had to make a positive difference in the lives of others. There is no more stifling feeling than knowing you have a big purpose, a big destiny, and feeling like you're failing to answer the calling. It is because of these experiences, these struggles, that I have become incredibly passionate about two things.

First, there is a very conscious order when it comes to building your business. If you do things in a conscious, and thorough sequence, you can bypass almost all of the struggles I went through. This doesn't mean if you haven't been doing this, you're doing something wrong, it just means that there is a whole new level of success and abundance waiting for you when you combine your actions with a higher level of consciousness.

Second, when you take the time, and honor yourself (and your clients) enough to actually put the right energetic and practical foundations in place the universe opens door after door for you. There is a time to just put things out there. We're not talking about getting things perfect here. What we are talking about is really making sure that you have a foundation in place that can actually support you in creating the level of wealth that is most authentic to you.

I believe that many businesses fail because they don't have the right foundation, or they do all of the right things, at all of the wrong times.

Uncover Your Individual & Transcendent Purpose

There are crappy days in business. Sorry! I'm all about being spiritual, positive, and diving into your affirmations when things get tough, but anyone who tells you that every day is going to be easy, it just flat lying to you. The other thing that you need to know is that you are sometimes going to have to take actions you don't feel like taking, on days when you don't feel like taking them. Otherwise you'll always be starting and stopping, which is one of the biggest enemies of success.

Rather than deluding yourself that you'll never have a day where you want to quit, or even worse that you can simply take a "time-out" every time you don't feel like implementing your business plan, a much better and more profitable alternative is to have a process in place that will allow you to navigate those difficult days.

I'm going to share one of the best ways that I know to move through the hard days in business with grace. It deals with what I call your "Individual Purpose" and your "Transcendent Purpose." I will explain the difference in just a moment, but for now know both are essential to taking consistent action and cultivating success, because without them you'll simply give up when the going gets tough. Or you'll listen to the voices of the naysayers and haters.

Wealth Alignment Principle: The universe opens door after door for those who act upon their purpose.

Many people simply describe this as your reason for starting your business, or your "Big Why" and that's certainly an OK way of describing this idea, but I actually want to take you to a deeper, more empowered place by breaking this down into two separate, and equally important, concepts: your individual purpose and your transcendent purpose.

Your Individual Purpose is your specific, personal reasons for starting your business. This is usually something like wanting to have more time to spend with your family, more money to put into your children's college fun, or more flexibility and resources to travel. Your Individual Purpose is the deeply personal reasons you have for wanting to be successful.

Acknowledging your Individual Purpose is important because it allows you to connect the dots between what you're doing to make money, and the direct effect of that on your life. If you're going to be an entrepreneur and start a business, instead of having a job, don't you want that business to afford you a lifestyle that you *absolutely* love living? I know I do!

Identifying your Individual Purpose also helps you avoid the martyrdom trap that so many conscious entrepreneurs fall into. There are so many wounded healers out there getting their self-esteem from making their lives hard, and saying over and over "I don't do this for myself." Or, "I don't do this for the money." Here's the bottom line: life is much, much harder when you don't have the level of success, and *yes* money, that you desire. When you are connected to your Individual Purpose you give yourself permission to acknowledge that it is wonderful to have a business, do something you love, and to have the this thing you love improve your life.

Map out your Individual Purpose in the space below:

_____

_____

_____

_____

_____

_____

_____

_____

_____

_____

_____

_____

_____

The other piece of the equation is your Transcendent Purpose. Every single conscious entrepreneur I have ever had the opportunity to meet, coach, and connect with has one. Your Transcendent Purpose is your big, global, planetary mission. It's what many of us think of as our calling. It's the reason we do what we do, that is so much bigger than ourselves. For some of you, this might be a social mission or charitable cause. For others it might deal with reorienting the way we've always done things, or always thought about things, on the planet.

My Transcendent Purpose deals with massively expanding the way we think about what's possible for our lives, transforming the way wealth is distributed on the planet, and ensuring that this generation of conscious entrepreneurs find ways to make their businesses profitable.

I'm passionate about expanding our definition of "meaningful work" because I see people every day march off to jobs that slowly kill their souls. Growing up I had no idea that being an "entrepreneur' was even an option! I'm passionate about transforming the way wealth is distributed on the planet because I believe that bringing opportunities to create wealth to those who have been denied these opportunities for too long is essential to elevating our planet by reducing economic scarcity, poverty, and war. And finally, I'm passionate about helping this generation of entrepreneurs figure out how to make their ventures profitable, because I believe that if we don't, the next generation, our children, will simply view starting these kind of businesses as foreclosed to them.

If you want to build a business that does big things, you have to be willing to aim high, to think big, and to constantly expand your definition of what's possible. Getting in touch with your big mission, the very thing that I believe you came to this planet to achieve, is part of that process.

Identifying your Transcendent Purpose is not for the faint of heart. It requires a lot of courage. You might be thinking, "Who am I do transform something *that* big?" The answer is: you're exactly the right person to do something that big. You wouldn't have even been drawn to start the businesses you're currently in if you weren't meant to do big things. Whether you do them or not, is up to you, but for now put that voice that tells you you're better off staying small out of your mind...

Dig deep...

Get into the present moment...

And take a minute or two to journal about your Transcendent Purpose

_____

_____

_____

_____

_____

_____

_____

_____

_____

_____

_____

_____

Are you starting to see how the combination of your Individual and Transcendent Purpose is powerful and necessary for long-term success? I recommend writing down both your Individual and Transcendent Purpose and putting them someplace where you will *be forced* to look at them each day. Anytime you get distracted, are tempted to not take action, or start to let your fear become more important to you than your success, re-read your Individual and Transcendent Purpose and get re-focused on your mission.

If you don't know the deeply personal, as well as the much bigger reasons why you're doing something, success isn't likely. Because when you are really crystal clear about the reasons why you are doing something, you realize it's unfair to you, and completely unfair to the people you could help, not to take the action that will bring your vision from a simple thought into reality.

Wealth Alignment Principle: When your mission matters more to you than your fear, success becomes inevitable.

When success doesn't occur all that happened is your fear, your desire to stay comfortable, or your present circumstances became more important to you than your Individual and Transcendent Purpose. When you are really centered on both your Individual and your Transcendent Purpose how can you not take action every single day toward your goals? You owe it to yourself and to the world to put the right plan in place, get powerful support, and take actions that are going to help you live your dreams.

Using Your Purpose and Your Vision to Navigate Tough Days

One of the things that happens when you commit to becoming successful through building a business that transforms lives, is that every single thing that isn't success, every single thing that isn't high vibration, and every single thing that could possibly sabotage your achieving that goal, comes to the surface. Negative thoughts, limiting beliefs, and old wounds come bubbling up. When you make a decision to shift one area of your life, you begin to notice every other area where you have work to do as well.

This doesn't happen to punish you. It's not the universe telling you that you're on the wrong path. Instead, your commitment to success signifies that you are *finally* serious about transforming your life and living your purpose, which is a hugely mature place to reach. All of these seemingly negative things are coming up because you have a new level of awareness from which to heal and move past them. I challenge you, as things come up that threaten to sabotage your success, to ask yourself, "What part of myself needs to be healed to allow me to turn this obstacle into an opportunity?"

Sometimes it's just a bad minute or a bad day, and other times we may feel funky for a few weeks at a time. I want you to know that this is completely normal. In fact, when we understand what's going on from a metaphysical and spiritual perspective we can see that it's actually a healthy process. We are being given the opportunity to release and heal all the things that will inhibit our transformation, and hence our joy.

The next Wealth Alignment Principle is an attempt to explain the transformational process your body, mind, and spirit go through when you make a serious commitment to change. Notice I said "explain" not "make completely easy, so that you never have one sad, tough, or difficult moment!"

Wealth Alignment Principle: There is always a major breakdown before a major breakthrough.

Spiritual work is always a two-part process: releasing the old and replacing it with the new. We might think of the old as that which served us at one time, but no longer. And we might think of the new as that which currently serves us, and will allow us to become the person necessary to receive our vision. It is impossible for transformation to occur if only one part of the process is undertaken. If you only release that which no longer serves you, without doing the work to adopt a new way of being, the old simply reconstitutes itself, often stronger than before. If you only focus on dumping a new way of thinking on top of old and damaging wounds, the old way of thinking slowly picks away at the new thoughts and beliefs like a cancer.

There's something very sad, almost tragic, that has occurred in the metaphysical community in the last couple of decades, which is that we've ignored the releasing part of the process, and focused all of our efforts on the replacing part. Don't believe me? Pick up any number of so-called-self-help-books that will tell you all of your problems can be magically solved by just repeating enough affirmations. Spirituality isn't about pretending, denying, or ignoring that negative thoughts, feelings, and beliefs exist. Sometimes we have as much to learn from facing these negative thoughts and really reconciling where they are coming from as we do from jumping into the positive and joyful sides of life.

At my annual live event Wealth Creation LIVE (http://www. wealthcreationliveevent.com if you're interested in attending), I spoke with a woman who was almost in tears because she had been repeating her affirmations thousands of times each day, and saw little changing in her life. As we explored what was going on, we uncovered that she was harboring a deep belief that success was just, "Never going to be a reality for her." Of course affirmations weren't going to work until she faced this incredibly harmful, uncomfortable, and damaging belief. That's like trying to plant a seed in infertile soil, in a place that gets zero sunlight, and then complaining at the seed because it wasn't able to flourish.

Of course we rush to the positive because it feels really good to hang out in the high-vibrating spiritual realm. The hard truth though is that sometimes we can use the spiritual realm: the realm of affirmations, the realm of visualizing, the realm of meditation etc., as a way to escape and avoid taking the daily actions we need to actually see our vision brought into reality.

The only way to begin releasing, and ultimately healing, something is to face it. I once had a branding and marketing consultant tell me that I shouldn't tell my clients this fact, and instead focus on all of the wonderful, positive, and thriving aspects of what I do. I promptly hung up the phone. Yes, it's true, there are going to be amazing moments where you thrive in your business, but there are also going to be moments where you have to walk through the fire. Those are the moments that really determine your character, and those are the moments that have been the greatest gifts to me in my entrepreneurial journey. Because once you transcend a particular obstacle or difficulty, if you've learned from it the next time it arises you deal with it quickly and without drama.

It's not easy to go through the breakdown part of this process, but the light on the other side makes it so much more than worth it. Because on the other side of the breakdown process we realize there are levels of grace, happiness, and satisfaction we didn't even know we were capable of experiencing. That is how the ego keeps us stuck, by convincing us not to transform because it might be worse. It's a lie. The deep spiritual truth is that there is a paradise waiting for you on the other side of chasm between what you believe you deserve and what you actually deserve.

One of the best ways I know to more quickly navigate the breakdowns is by using a simple two-part process. First, simply introduce the Wealth Alignment Principle into your consciousness by saying, "I'm feeling a breakdown, and even though it's painful, I have faith that it is the precursor to an amazing transformation." Second, print out your Individual and Transcendent Purpose and read them frequently during the difficult times. Remember your deeply personal and spiritual reasons for pursuing entrepreneurship.

For me, taking time to consciously remember *why it is* I do what I do, has been the miracle cure to inaction, passivity and fear. It doesn't lessen the pain of dealing with the difficult days, but it does allow you to take inspired action anyway.

Crafting Your Energetic Business Plan

What I'm going to share with you next, I am so proud of, because I believe it perfectly encapsulates the approach I take in all of my coaching programs which is to combine practical action with powerful energetic techniques, allowing you to create success, live your purpose, and make an impact quickly and meaningfully. For a fuller, and more complete version of this exercise please go to http://www.consciousguidebookgifts.com.

For now, I'm going to explain the exercise to you, and then give you the express version. It is my belief that just as we create endless practical plans, action steps, and to-do lists to keep us on task, we must also create energetic or vision plans to help ensure every action we take is infused with inspiration and purpose. How often do we focus on taking actions while never pausing to think, "What in the heck am I actually doing this for?" Or how often do we know that we want things to change, but we lack clarity around what those changes would actually look like?

Now that you know your purpose, you're already starting to notice deep subtle shifts that are unlocking your inner power. The next part of the process is to gain crystal clear clarity around your vision, your goals, and what you want to achieve. I believe that just by mapping out our ultimate vision two things begin to happen. First, we actually give ourselves permission to have it. Second, we give the universe instructions on what we would like delivered to us. The universe responds to these two shifts by starting to rewire our lives, and our inner being, in such a way that actually receiving this vision becomes possible.

Action without vision is meaningless, and vision without action is meaningless, and it's often the reason we don't get the results we want. We either have vision without action, or we have action without vision. In Chapter Four, we'll deal with taking action. In this Chapter, we're going to deal with putting the vision component in place.

Think of your vision as the exact way you would like your life and business constructed to bring you the most fulfillment, joy, and satisfaction. One of the most effective ways to map out your vision is by creating what I call an Energetic Business Plan.

If you could step into your perfect business tomorrow, what would it be like? How would you feel? What would the environment be like? How many hours would you work? What is the ultimate, end goal of creating your business? How many more people would you help? What charities would you give to?

This is just some of the information you are going to connect with in crafting your Energetic Business Plan. On any given day there are so many different actions you have the choice to take. Not to mention on any given day there are so many different distractions that can prevent you from taking action. If you want to be successful you need a decision making sieve, a way of knowing which actions are the most important to take right now, and which actions would be better shelved for a later date.

Success comes from consistently taking those actions which are most in alignment with your vision. One of the best ways I know to figure out what those actions are is by using your Energetic Business Plan because it allows you to clearly see which actions are going to support the conscious creation of your vision, and which actions are merely distractions or activities you're engaging in because they are comfortable.

For example, if you determine in mapping out your Energetic Business Plan, that you would like to spend most of your time seeing clients and directly delivering your services to those clients, then an immediate action you might want to take is to fill your calendar up with conversations with potential clients who would be a good fit for what your business offers. Instead of deciding to spend your day updating your Facebook page, changing the colors on your websites, or investing in pay-per-click advertising.

Filling up your calendar with good conversations with solid leads might be uncomfortable, it's true, but it's the action that is more in alignment with your vision than hiding out behind your computer. Crafting your Energetic Business Plan isn't about giving you the easiest actions to take, it's about giving you the aligned actions, that when consistently implemented, will rocket you to the next level of success and wealth.

Let's jump into the Energetic Business Plan Exercise. Begin by answering the following set of questions. Remember, because this is your personalized plan, it's important to not overthink your answers, and to really answer from your heart.

My ultimate vision for my business looks like...

_____

_____

_____

_____

_____

_____

_____

_____

_____

_____

_____

_____

How am I treated and/or perceived differently when I achieve this vision...

_____

_____

_____

_____

_____

_____

_____

_____

_____

_____

_____

_____

I would like to spend most of my time doing this in my business...

_____

_____

_____

But I actually spend the most time doing this in my business...

_____

_____

_____

The one thing that I need to change/shift the most in my business right now is...

_____

_____

_____

In my ideal business I make $_____ each year

In what area do you most need to shift the energy of your business to attract more wealth and success? Your attitude toward clients? Your attitude toward technology? Your thoughts about money? Your thoughts about yourself? Your

feelings of unworthiness? Be as specific and detailed as possible.

_____

_____

_____

_____

_____

_____

_____

_____

Describe an ideal day in your business. Would you see clients? Would you lead a workshop? Would you see corporate clients? Would you be speaking to large groups of people? Would you have time for leisure? Would you rely more heavily on your team? Describe in as much detail as possible your ultimate business vision.

_____

_____

_____

_____

_____

_____

_____

_____

_____

_____

_____

_____

_____

Considering everything you have just been brave enough to write about, devise a few strategies to bring a new, more prosperous energy, to your business.

_____

_____

_____

_____

_____

_____

_____

_____

_____

_____

_____

_____

Take a few minutes to re-read what you've written, and really allow it to sink in at deep levels. I recommend printing out this plan so you can look at it regularly. Anything you regularly give good, focused attention to begins to become your reality. When you are stuck or confused about which action you need to take next re-read your Energetic Business Plan and select the action that is most in line with helping you achieve this vision.

Whew! Take a deep breath. If you're reading this, and you've *actually* done the exercises, you probably feel like you've just ridden the emotional roller coaster of personal development. Good! That's the point! Even though I know it can be uncomfortable, really evaluating your purpose, your vision, and crafting a plan for what you actually want to create is some of the most important work you can do. Especially when it comes to giving you the advantage of achieving success in your business.

So many entrepreneurs neglect this work because they are afraid to confidently stand behind their vision, thinking, "Who am I to do this work?" Laying a foundation that encompasses both what you practically want to achieve and why it is spiritually important for you to do so is going to allow you to take action long after other people have given up, gone back to a day job, or become content blaming the world, the economy, or something else for why they can't be successful.

CHAPTER THREE

The Wealthy Entrepreneur

I wanted to title this Chapter everything you need to know, do and commit to, if you want to own a highly profitable, highly successful business, but it seemed a bit too long. You might be wondering why I chose to focus this book toward entrepreneurs. The short answer is because a huge percentage of entrepreneurs will never cross the six-figure mark in their business, and a huge segment of those entrepreneurs desperately want to do so. I believe the reason for most entrepreneurs playing relatively small has almost nothing to do with marketing and almost everything to do with mindset. Thus, I wrote a guidebook to wealth for entrepreneurs.

The longer answer is because I believe deeply that the gifts possessed by entrepreneurs hold the key to the salvation of our planet. The potential of business owners and entrepreneurs to do business in a conscious way holds tremendous potential for social and planetary transformation. The messages I hear conscious entrepreneurs sharing with their clients every single day are truly transformational. It breaks my heart when one of these amazing entrepreneurs has to give up on their vision or go and get a job because they don't know how to create wealth in their businesses.

If socially conscious and spiritual entrepreneurs don't figure out how to play bigger – the world pays the price. If this generation of healers doesn't figure out how to make being a spiritual entrepreneur a profitable venture, then the next generation simply won't view it as a viable career path and transformational entrepreneurism will die. This generation of entrepreneurs will determine whether business stays stuck in its old regimented and profit-only mentality, or whether it will evolve and become a force for conscious good rather than destruction.

Conversely, I believe that everyone wins when spiritual and conscious entrepreneurs become truly wealthy. You win because you get to rock out your life in exactly the way you want. Your clients win because you are able to hold a space for them to do the same, while showing up with so much more to give. The world wins because we are able to use your newfound position of wealth to give more to improve it.

Conscious entrepreneurism may be the single greatest force for reshaping the world into a place that reflects a better, more empowered, more peaceful, more loving set of values. It also has the potential to reshape the way we think about work and employment by allowing a set of jobs to be created in which workers are respected, and truly made a part of a team, rather than viewed as commodities to be exploited for their productivity. For any of this to happen, these businesses must be profitable.

Wealth Alignment Principle: Money is simply an energy that can be harnessed to bring a vision into reality.

There are lots of other energies required to bring a vision into reality, including dedication, commitment, structure, goals, deadlines, and the list goes on. But money is an essential energy if you are to bring your vision to the world. Money is often the energy that allows you to be able to bring your vision to a much bigger audience than was previously available to you. It is also the energy that allows you to bring in the right collaborators, and build the necessary team.

Saying that money is energy is the same thing as saying energy has a vibration. Which means that if you want to create more of it you must raise your vibration. I'll be giving you a lot of techniques to be able to do this throughout the book. For now, it's just important to understand that money is neither good nor bad, it's the orientation of the person with the money that determines its value.

If you had unlimited money what vision would you bring into reality?

_____

_____

_____

_____

_____

_____

_____

_____

_____

_____

_____

_____

_____

Spend several minutes connecting deeply with this vision. Allow yourself to feel emotionally connected to the vision. Too often we let the stories we were told growing up, from our parents, from our religions, from our circumstances determine how we feel about money. We create particular beliefs around money either good or bad. Money becomes either something evil to be avoided or something God-like to be revered.

What stories were you told about money growing up? How does viewing money as an energy to fuel your success come into conflict with these views?

_____

_____

_____

_____

_____

_____

_____

_____

_____

_____

_____

_____

_____

How will shifting your view of money from something with inherent value to a force to fuel your success and your vision allow you to write a more productive money story moving forward?

_____

_____

_____

_____

_____

_____

_____

_____

_____

The Marketing Trap: Medium versus Message

As an entrepreneur you know that a huge part of whether or not you are successful at growing your business lies in your ability to effectively market your business. One thing I hear all of the time from entrepreneurs, especially entrepreneurs who may be more sensitive or intuitive by nature, is that they don't like marketing their businesses. Or they find marketing hard. Another variation of this is, "I wish someone else could handle my marketing for me."

If this is the type of energy that you are putting into your marketing, is it really any wonder you aren't getting the results you want? I've learned that the level of consciousness at which I undertake a project has everything to do with the results I get. Are clients going be drawn to someone who brings the energy of arrogance or resistance to their marketing? Or are they going to want to work with someone who is authentic and shows up fully and powerfully in their marketing?

Most entrepreneurs don't succeed at marketing their business because they think the power lies in the medium. By this I mean, that we overvalue "how" we market rather than considering the message both apparent, and beneath the surface, that we are conveying.

The power to grow your business and make money doesn't lie in the medium. It doesn't matter whether you use video marketing, blogging, social media marketing, in person or online networking, article writing, webinars, teleconferences, joint venture relationships, workshops, speaking or any other medium to grow your business. All of these can work fantastically, or not so fantastically, if they are inauthentic to you. The power to grow your business through marketing, which also means your power to transform lives through your business, lies in a powerful message that is attuned to a particular audience. I think of this in spiritual terms. Success in marketing comes from understanding the exact divine message we are here to share with the exact divine audience.

Wealth Alignment Principle: Your unique energetic essence, which is already contained within you, holds enormous wealth potential.

We'll deal with finding your divine right audience in a moment. Uncovering your divine marketing message requires you to get in touch with what makes you, you. Too often in marketing we try to copy what someone else is doing, or model ourselves off of the people we admire. Instead, we need to give ourselves permission to grow our business, and market ourselves in a way that works with, rather than against, who we are. This is where the concept of your unique energetic essence comes into play.

I believe everyone has a unique energetic essence, something about them that makes them absolutely unique, and suited for the work they are meant to do on this planet. It doesn't matter if you're an entrepreneur or not, this essence is contained within you. What's unique about the entrepreneur's journey is that we can actually tap into this unique energetic essence, and share it with the world through our marketing.

Wealthy entrepreneurs have a point of view, and even when they are afraid, they share that point of view with the world. Unsuccessful entrepreneurs also have a point of view they just either aren't fully connected with it or don't have the courage to express it in the world.

We are often told as children that while we are special, it's arrogant to really be honest and express that specialness in the world. Don't be too special, too smart, too talented, you might offend someone, or make someone else feel bad. Nonsense. We came to this planet as divine, spiritual beings with unique missions, and we cannot complete those missions if we are disconnected from our power, our authenticity, and our uniqueness.

I'm going to take you through an exercise that will help you connect with your unique energetic essence. You can use this to refine and hone your marketing message, but also to simply get connected to those parts of yourself that you've made not good enough, denied, or repressed.

What makes you...you? What is unique about you?

What is unique about the way you work and the way you do business?

_____

_____

_____

_____

_____

_____

_____

_____

_____

_____

_____

_____

_____

Imagine that you have just served a client and they are extremely happy with the work you've done for them. Write a testimonial, from their perspective, about their experience of working with you.

_____

_____

_____

_____

_____

_____

_____

_____

_____

_____

_____

_____

I want you to look at everything you've just written about your unique essence. Is this essence reflected in your marketing copy? On your website? In the way you are communicating with your customers?

My guess? Probably not. If you aren't having the success you want, it's almost always because not enough of you is showing up in the way you are doing business. Connecting to what makes us, and the way we do business, unique is one of the most powerful ways we have to neutralize the advantage of mega-brands with huge advertising budgets and gigantic public relations infrastructure.

Think about that for just a minute? You have all of the resources you need, contained within you, to build a profitable, thriving business. You can show up exactly as you are, armed only with your God-given abilities, talents, and your genuine desire to serve, and watch as big time results are created. This uniqueness combined with the ability of our customers to relate to us directly and intimately results in a powerful alchemical mixture that is critical to wealth and success.

Everything about me that I was told was a liability growing up: my inability to focus on just one project, my obsessive desire to start new things, my innate sensitivities and intuitive ability, and my willingness to try a new way of doing things, turned out to be the greatest assets I had to be able to create wealth in my life! The same is true for you. Those things you've been told make you outside the norm, are actually divine gifts that when harnessed effectively will result in magic beyond your wildest dream.

Of course whether you connect with these divine gifts and use them to create wealth, or whether you choose to believe the story that you need to be normal and do things like everyone else is really up to you. Some people spend their entire life trying to conform to what they think they should be. My advice: don't be one of them.

It can be scary to reveal your unique essence to the world. Especially because we spend large chunks of our lives trying to keep ourselves hidden because people have been unkind or ungentle with us and we fear they will do it again. Revealing who we really are can be scary enough when we're revealing it to people we know and trust, let alone putting it out there publicly in a big way.

This is why it is so important to take the focus off of ourselves and put it back onto the people we are really meant to serve. Consider this:

If you were able to give someone else permission to play big, to be themselves, and to unleash their unique essence in the world, would it be worth walking through your fears?

This is not about splashing your energy and personal life over your clients and customers. It's not about revealing every single private detail of your life to the world. Rather, it's about making it easy for clients to get to know you. It's about letting them know that you are a real person with real ups and downs, who really cares about their transformation.

It's also important to remember that you only need to feel safe enough to take the first step. Remember the virtue of being uncomfortable! This is not about feeling completely comfortable, this is about making yourself comfortable enough to begin to put yourself out there, so you can make more money, and serve more clients.

Sometimes we keep ourselves stuck by thinking we need every single thing to be in place to take the first step, instead of focusing on how we can make ourselves feel safe enough to take courageous action.

With this in mind, what would it take for you to feel safe revealing your unique essence to the world?

_____

_____

_____

_____

_____

_____

_____

_____

_____

_____

_____

_____

_____

_____

Now that you feel safe, what action step will you commit to implementing this week that allows your unique essence to become known and seen in your business?

_____

_____

_____

_____

_____

_____

_____

_____

_____

_____

_____

_____

_____

_____

Find Your Audience, Find Your Wealth

Doesn't it feel great to give yourself permission to just be you? Doesn't it feel great to know that you get to create your business working with the essence of who you are, instead of trying to be something you're not? Of course it does! Because the universe gifted you with everything you need to be able to create wealth. We're born with the guidebook. We're born with the exact unique gifts that we need to be able to manifest money, wealth, and riches. It's everything else that happens after we're born that convinces us that this isn't true.

Now it's time to discover exactly WHO you are meant to serve. Not only do you have a divine unique essence, you also have a divine audience that you are divinely equipped to serve. In traditional business or marketing terminology this is often referred to as your target market or your niche market, both of which sound somewhat dispassionate to me. I prefer instead to think of this unique group of people that you are uniquely qualified to serve as your divine client audience.

Wealth Alignment Principle: Solve specific problems, for specific groups of people, and wealth will follow.

Your divine client audience is made up of those specific individuals for whom you solve a specific problem or help them achieve a particular aspiration or transformation. Your ability to connect deeply with this audience is directly related to how much money you make.

Your divine client audience will satisfy three conditions.

1. *Your divine client audience will be aware that they need what you offer.*

2. *Your divine client audience will gather in common spaces, both online and offline, that make them accessible to you.*

3. *Your divine client audience will be willing to invest money for your services or products.*

Too many entrepreneurs neglect doing the work of identifying their divine client audience mistakenly believing they are meant to help absolutely everyone. While this comes from a well meaning part of us, the part that wants to help a lot of people, refusing to find our divine client audience actually keeps us safe, playing small, and unable to reach the individuals that we were actually put on this planet to help.

I can hear the objections now:

I'll exclude someone

I'll leave someone out

I'll have to turn clients away

I'll get more people with a broad focus

I have gifts that can help anyone regardless of their problem

This is your ego trying to prevent you from connecting with the unique audience that you are super-duper qualified to help. When you know exactly who you serve and exactly what problem you help them solve or aspiration you help them achieve you end up serving more, not less, people. In fact, not choosing a specific audience actually sabotages the success of your business and the growth of your client base.

When you aren't clear on who your divine client audience is, your marketing remains generic, uninteresting, and ephemeral. It doesn't give clients something concrete and meaningful to grasp onto. While clients might find your message interesting, very rarely will they take the next step and feel an emotional pull to work with you, because they simply can't understand what it is that you offer.

If you don't know whom you are writing your marketing for, it leaves you writing marketing copy that is vague and unspecific. This leaves potential clients confused about if you can actually help them. If you're a business coach and a client logs onto your website because they want to grow their business and make more money, and your marketing copy says you help people "find happiness and inner peace" you risk a client clicking off your website because they don't think that you can help them with the problem they have. If you're a weight loss coach, and instead of talking about helping people lose weight and feel better, you choose to talk about "achieving a state of inner bliss" you're risking losing clients that you are uniquely suited to help because they think you solve a different problem than the one they have.

In short, how can you compose marketing copy that makes any sense without knowing exactly who that copy is designed to appeal to? By being vague and unspecific you actually have the opposite of the intended effect. Instead of helping more people, you end up making it impossible for potential clients to know if you are the person to help them.

One of the biggest practical problems of not knowing your divine client audience is that clients simply can't find you. Why? Because clients don't look for someone to help them with every single problem they have. Instead, they look for specific people to help them with specific problems. When you try and help absolutely everyone you make it difficult for your clients to find you.

Any divine client audience that you choose is going to be comprised of thousands of individuals who need your help. Most likely any viable divine client audience is going to have more people than you could possibly help in your entire lifetime. When you get specific, and you're willing to courageously say "This is the group of people I came here to serve," you end up helping more people and making it easy for potential clients to make the decision that YES you are the person to work with.

Your divine client audience can certainly change, shift, and evolve over time. You may also add additional divine client audiences to your business as you grow and expand. The key here is not about limiting yourself, boxing yourself in, or prohibiting you from working with certain clients, rather, it's about building up one arm of your business, and after that arm of your business is successful growing and adding additional client audiences as it supports your bigger mission and your bigger vision in the world.

When I began my business, I worked only with entrepreneurs earning less than 50,000 dollars a year. The reason? I was completely confident that I could help this group of entrepreneurs. As I grew and expanded it became clear to me that I was also meant to help already successful entrepreneurs embody more fully into their purpose and vision. So I added an additional divine client audience. It was much easier to do this after already having established a successful practice helping struggling entrepreneurs. Had I tried to work with all of these people in the beginning it would have been incredibly time consuming, and it would have prevented me from having big success quickly because my focus would have been split.

Start with one viable and specific divine client audience, and add additional client audiences as it makes sense to do so. If you start working with one client audience, and it isn't working for you, simply choose another client audience. Sometimes it takes more than one try for us to figure out who is simply a client audience and who is really our divine tribe.

Are you ready to discover your divine client audience? Are you ready to uncover the exact group of people that you are meant to serve at this moment in your business? I'm going to take you through an exercise to help you do just that. You may want to go through this exercise a couple of times, come up with a few potential divine client audiences, and compare which one really feels right for you to work with at this time.

Would you prefer to serve (primarily) men or women? Or doesn't matter? (Circle)

Men.   Women.   Both.   Doesn't Matter.

What age ranges would you most like to work with?

1-10   10-15 15-19 20-35 35-50   50-65 65+

What similarities exist between the individuals that you currently serve?

_____

_____

_____

_____

_____

_____

_____

_____

_____

_____

_____

_____

_____

What group(s) of individuals do you have an overwhelming desire to serve?

_____

_____

_____

_____

_____

_____

_____

_____

_____

_____

_____

_____

_____

What qualities would you like your ideal clients to have?

_____

_____

_____

_____

_____

_____

_____

_____

_____

_____

_____

_____

Which groups of individuals are you best suited to serve based on your existing talents, skills, credentials, qualifications, or life experience?

_____

_____

_____

_____

_____

_____

_____

_____

_____

_____

_____

_____

What problems do your clients most consistently seek you out to help them solve? Be specific!

_____

_____

_____

_____

_____

_____

_____

_____

_____

_____

_____

_____

_____

If you had a steady stream of clients tomorrow, what problem would you be the most excited to help them solve?

_____

_____

_____

_____

_____

_____

_____

_____

_____

_____

_____

_____

Based on your previous answers, without overthinking, which group of individuals would you most like to serve right now?

My divine client audience is _____

Congratulations! You've just discovered your divine client audience. If you don't feel comfortable with it yet, that's OK. Sometimes you need to take a couple of days and come back to this exercise. Next up, I'm going to walk you through how to create tremendous value for this audience so that they can't wait to engage with you.

Don't be a Copy Cat

Your job after identifying your divine client audience is to deliver tremendous value to them in the form of your programs, products or services. There's a difference between delivering "great" value and delivering "greatest" value. I want every single one of my clients, customers, JV partners, and prospects to feel that I delivered them the absolute greatest value possible.

A lot of you reading this are delivering "great" value right now to your clients, but you probably aren't delivering "greatest" value. I say this because so often when we begin in business we are doing things because we think we "should" or because we see other people doing them, rather than because they are truly authentic and the right thing for us to do. Anytime we are trying to copy or mirror another person we are not delivering the greatest value to our clients.

Wealth Alignment Principle: Money loves originality. When you are authentic and original, you become a money magnet.

This impulse to mirror, copy, and duplicate what other people are doing is a reaction to a deep inner fear most of us hold. The fear that just being who we are isn't good enough. Surely we have to mold, change, and twist ourselves into a perfect professional entrepreneur if we want to own a profitable business, the ego tells us. In short order, all of our greatest assets are repressed because someone out in the world might find them unappealing. Your amazing sense of humor, your ability to be blunt and direct, or your unique fashion sense gets traded in, and what emerges is a completely safe, completely uninteresting business owner .

We become mirror images of other entrepreneurs when we are not clear about our unique spiritual gifts. Usually, it's because we neglect whatever comes easy to us. I hear people say all the time, "Oh that comes so naturally to me, it can't possibly be something that would help me create wealth." Here's the truth: that which comes easiest to you, is your divine gift, and has the greatest potential to draw money, success, and wealth toward you. Instead of working against these gifts, by trying to become something you're not, start working with them, and watch as money starts to flow in more easily.

Unfortunately, in my view, too many business and marketing coaches and consultants unwittingly perpetuate this system of copying and duplicating with all their talk about "proven systems."

"If you just do a, and then b, and then c...." I'm sure you've seen this on many different sales pages, marketing copy, or perhaps you've even been told it directly by one of these coaches or consultants. It's not that the system didn't work for them, and it's not that there isn't great wisdom, and information contained within this system, it's just that if you are not infusing these systems with your unique energetic essence the chance that you'll really get the results you want is pretty low.

I view my role as an intuitive business mentor, as being able to create a space from which your greatness can easily emerge, and then educate you about those marketing and sales systems that are really going to support you in having the kind of life you want.

I'm all for having great systems and structures in place in your business that support your growth, money making potential, and creativity. What I'm not all about is implementing another coach's exact system and expecting to get the exact same results. Systems put in place because they worked for someone else are not likely to yield results. Systems that are infused with your unique energetic essence, put in place because they support the kind of life you truly desire, make magic happen. Have the courage to architect your business in a way that truly serves your soul.

The impulse to duplicate has real, and serious, consequences on your bottom line. I want to give you a couple of examples of how this plays out. The first example deals with how we package and deliver our services or products. As entrepreneurs, too often we deliver our programs, products, and services in the way that other people are delivering them instead of stretching ourselves to discover what is the way that we can deliver our services in a way that provides the "greatest" value. If you aren't having the success you want in your business, perhaps it's because instead of doing what is really true and right for you, you're copying the way others are doing it.

One common mistake that healers, coaches, and intuitives make all of the time is delivering their services on a per session basis, instead of enrolling their clients into longer-term work with them. When you charge on a per session basis, you're charging for time, which limits what you can charge pretty quickly. Why? People are simply unwilling to pay high amounts of money for someone's time...including yours. Think about it? What's the most you would pay someone for an hour of time.

When you enroll your clients into a package, where you work with them over a number of weeks or months, you're not charging for time, instead you're charging for the results that you deliver. People are willing to pay a lot more money for results than they are for time. Not to mention if people work with you longer, and invest more with you, the results they get will be much bigger and much more sustainable.

This is just one example of where you might be structuring your business in a certain way because others are doing it that way, rather than really focusing on how you can uniquely deliver profound value to your clients and customers. Another place I see this all the time is when it comes to pricing your programs, products, and services. Especially when it comes to helping professionals and entrepreneurs there is a knee jerk reaction that encourages us just to look at what other people are doing, and then price our services accordingly.

Since a huge percentage of entrepreneurs fail, or only ever create limited success in their business, if you're copying what other people are doing, you're most likely copying an unsuccessful model. Even if you go to the top people in your industry, people who are clearly successful, that doesn't mean the way they do things is going to be authentic and work for you.

There are only two things I consider when I price any program that I'm going to offer.

1. What is the investment that a client needs to make to *really* take this seriously and get results?

2. If I accept the transformation as a forgone conclusion, what is that transformation worth to someone?

That's it. I don't worry about what other coaches are charging. I don't have anxiety about what clients might be willing to pay for a certain transformation. I don't obsess over whether people will be able to afford it. I don't doubt my skills or ability to deliver the transformation to people who implement the program.

Let's take a hard look at where you've sacrificed your own originality and authenticity to follow along with the crowd.

Identify at least 3 places in your business where you're doing things because you think you should, rather than because they really resonate with you.

1. _____

2. _____

3. _____

Where in your business are you doing things because you think you should, rather than because it really serves your clients, your customers, or you?

_____

_____

_____

_____

_____

_____

_____

_____

_____

_____

_____

_____

_____

If you had the courage to run the business you really want to own, instead of the one you think you're supposed to own, what would a typical day look like?

_____

_____

_____

_____

_____

_____

_____

_____

_____

_____

_____

_____

_____

What change can you make today to start bringing yourself into alignment with this vision?

_____

_____

_____

_____

_____

_____

_____

_____

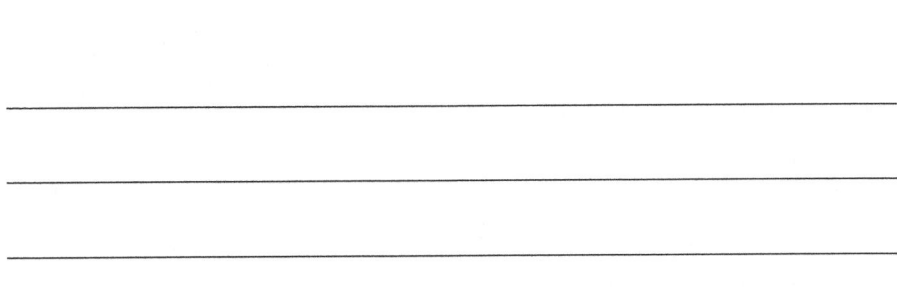

What would be different for you if you knew exactly what your life-changing message was, who you were meant to serve, and how to present that message to your ideal client audience in a way that got them excited about working with you? My guess is everything. Many entrepreneurs never take the actions mentioned in this Chapter, because they stay stuck in fear, doubt, and self-sabotage. In the following Chapters, we'll deal with how you can move through these mental, emotional, and spiritual obstacles. This is where so many marketing and business-building books fall short. They give you great information, and tactics, but they fail to give you the energetic shifts necessary to actually be able to implement the information.

It takes courage to go out into the world authentically and powerfully. If it were easy you wouldn't be reading this book. However, it is the only aligned choice for entrepreneurs who really want to help people and make a difference with their work. If you choose to show-up in the world in a way that isn't authentic, powerful, and in alignment with your purpose you won't create sustainable wealth, experience deep levels of fulfillment, and you will never help those individuals who are desperately seeking the transformation you provide.

CHAPTER FOUR

The Power of Right Action

I s it becoming clear to you by now that every excuse you have for not taking action in your business is really just the ego's way of keeping you safe, comfortable, and, in many cases, poor? If not, allow that to become clear now. We came to this planet as incredibly powerful beings, that simply by virtue of having a human experience, possess the potential to make an enormous positive impact on the world around us. Anytime we are not making choices and decisions, or taking action, from that awareness we are operating from a place of untruth that ultimately results in a feeling of deep disappointment.

Wealth Alignment Principle: Taking action for the sake of taking action is pointless. Taking action in service of your vision is the energy that will line the road to your ultimate happiness.

We've arrived at a particular moment in time where "The Secret" and the Law of Attraction nonsense has gotten completely out of hand. "The Secret" and the Law of Attraction are not nonsense at all, of course, they are powerful principles that, when conjoined with action, allow your life to unfold in an almost magical way. At some point, unfortunately, these principles got reduced to, "I can sit on my ass, make a vision board, and the universe will deliver me health, happiness, riches, and the perfect relationship."

I literally have entrepreneurs tell me that they don't need my help in creating a marketing or sales plan, and developing a systematic structure in their business, because they are reading a book on manifesting. Or they refuse to attend events and workshops that could educate them about marketing or sales, because in their words, they're going to wait for "Spirit to send the clients to them."

If you can't tell, this kind of thinking drives me absolutely crazy. It's laced with arrogance, and it turns the Law of Attraction and spirituality into an excuse for not taking action. The consequence of this for conscious entrepreneurs is that the people who need your help never get it. Can you imagine telling someone that you couldn't be bothered to go out and help them because you were too busy waiting for Spirit to send them to you? "Oh sorry I didn't go to that networking event, I was too busy meditating and asking the universe to send me clients."

The Law of Attraction is powerful when you orient yourself in a powerful way toward that which you desire to attract, and then take the action necessary to actually allow it to be made manifest in your life. Action is the way the universe delivers you the opportunities to enable you to be able to create your vision.

Which brings up a critical point about manifesting, a point that is curiously and unfortunately largely missing from much of the contemporary literature that hypes the Law of Attraction. You don't manifest things. You manifest opportunities. Whether you say "Yes" or whether you say "No" to those opportunities is entirely up to you.

Let me share a story with you from my own life that illustrates what I'm talking about. I've always been a spiritual seeker, and from the moment I stumbled into the "New Age" and "Self-Help" section of our local bookstore I was hooked. The writings of Marianne Williamson, Deepak Chopra, and many others moved me profoundly, and shifted my life in many positive ways. I started to understand that I was worth much more than I had previously known.

When I began my business, it was because I wanted to be someone who was able to help people in as equally profound a way. For years, I struggled to get the clients and make the money that I wanted. I would help people here and there, on a per session basis, work two, sometimes three jobs to get by, and constantly wonder when I was going to be able to make the income I wanted from my business.

Being a student of spirituality, manifesting, and the Law of Attraction, I would spend hours visualizing, meditating, and affirming what I wanted to create in my life: more money, more clients, more wealth, and most importantly, the ability to make a much bigger impact through my work. No matter how much spiritual work I did, it just didn't seem to be happening. Eventually I started to feel like I was failing at my spiritual practice because the external conditions of my life weren't matching my inner state.

During this failed manifesting process, a business coach came along and told me how she could support me in making more money, getting more clients, and in growing my business. I told her I couldn't afford to hire her, but I really appreciated her time. I went back to my meditating, visualization, and affirmation, desperately asking for the universe to send me the things I desired.

A few months later, a different business consultant came along, and again told me how she could help me grow my business, and get the things I wanted. Again, I told her that I couldn't afford to hire a business coach. I remember being adamant about it. "There's absolutely no way I could pay *that* kind of money." This time I was actually angry. "Who does she think she is, to charge rates like that!" I angrily exclaimed to a friend over a glass of chardonnay.

Are you starting to see what I didn't? My manifesting had actually been working the entire time! It was sending me opportunity after opportunity to gain the education and develop the skillset necessary to actually be able to get more clients, make more money, create more wealth, and make the impact that I so desperately desired to make. Instead of taking advantage of these opportunities, I turned them away confused about why, despite my best efforts, nothing seemed to change.

One month later, I connected with another business mentor, and this time something in me shifted. I realized, so clearly, that my way of doing things hadn't worked, and it was time to try something different. When the time came to discuss the investment price, I started to panic and resist. Thankfully, this time, a deeper voice inside me took over, and let me know that if I just took this first step everything would be OK.

I called my (now) husband and asked him for the two thousand dollars I would need to put the deposit down to work this amazing woman, something I had *never* done before. Even though I was scared, and even though I was embarrassed to have to ask him for the money, I was willing to move through those worries because figuring out a way to be successful and to help more people was more important to me than the fear.

I finally said yes to the opportunity that I had been putting so much mental, emotional, and spiritual energy into creating. One month later I achieved my first $10,000 month. Sixty days later I had my first $15,000 month. And just a little over six months later my first $25,000 month. Making a decision, and choosing to be supported instead of choosing to be in struggle, even though it was incredibly scary, transformed my business and my life.

Saying yes and taking definitive action toward my vision did something else for me that was more valuable than all of the money in the world. It shifted something inside of me, by showing me how tenacious, talented, resourceful and creative I really was. Instead of being a victim to my circumstances, I chose to be a courageous warrior to my commitment of building a business that makes a profound, positive difference in the lives of others. It cemented my belief in taking powerful action in my business every single day, and it led me to the next Wealth Alignment Principle.

Wealth Alignment Principle: Taking inspired action is the way the universe has given you to create the opportunities to actualize all that you can visualize. It is the vehicle you take to your vision, while visualization, meditation, desire, and Law of Attraction are the fuel.

Transformation is never more than a single decision away. In the instant we make the decision to transform our business, or really any area of our life, opportunities begin to show up that allow us to do so. Does this mean you decide to transform and then you have everything you've ever wanted? No. It means at any moment you have the power to make a singular aligned decision, which is the decision to truly and authentically ask for transformation. This decision sets in motion the exact string of events necessary to mold you into the person who is capable of receiving the transformation you desire. Let me illustrate how this works:

If we ask for our anger to be transformed into peace, situations that trigger us will show up, offering us the opportunity to practice compassion, forgiveness and graciousness instead.

If we ask to transform a particular relationship, everything that isn't working in that relationship will come to the surface, giving us an opportunity to process and deal with it as mature adults.

If we ask to transform our business, opportunity after opportunity will present itself to us to learn and be supported in marketing, sales, and business growth.

Whether or not we take these opportunities is entirely up to us. The universe doesn't care one way or another. It's not giving us a test. If we choose to say no to one opportunity, we may not have what we want, but there are always additional opportunities to take advantage of. When we say no over and over again to opportunities that would lead us to the life we desire, the problem is not that the universe stops presenting these opportunities to us. On the contrary, each day is resplendent with opportunities to improve your life. The problem is we start to lose our capacity to perceive and take advantage of these opportunities, because we have not built our "opportunity awareness muscle." We become blind to the possibility of transformation, and start to experience the world as a harsh and cruel place, rather than as a matrix of possibilities.

When you understand the truth that transformation can never be more than one single decision away, the only thing that can ever stand between you and what you desire is a decision to believe untruth. Untruth can be incredibly powerful, and it frequently takes the form of myths that we choose to tell ourselves and buy into. Usually these myths begin with, "I'd like to, but I can't..."

I call these myths the "Unsuccess Myths." Let's look closely at three of the myths we often believe that keep us from consciously creating the level of wealth we desire.

Unsuccess Myth #1: The Divine Timing Myth

For those of us that are spiritually minded, one of the concepts we're introduced to is the idea of divine timing. It's certainly an idea I resonate with very strongly as I look back on my life and start to connect the dots as to why difficult experiences and situations occurred. In retrospect, it becomes clear that everything I've gone through in my life occurred at exactly the right moment it needed to in order to propel me forward. This is not to say all of those experiences were enjoyable, but rather if we are open to learning from our good, as well as our bad experiences, we are able to connect the dots and perceive a greater meaning for all of the things we have courageously lived through.

You might think of the idea of divine timing as looking at the world in such a way that understands things occur when they need to rather than we desire them to. I also look at divine timing as explaining to us that different experiences, both difficult and joyful, occur because they are shaping us into the people we are meant to become, and they are providing us with opportunities to choose love, grace, and forgiveness. Unfortunately, as often happens with deep spiritual truths, there is a tendency to reduce them to spiritual clichés, that rather than illuminate and inspire, are used to excuse and justify the choices we've made.

This happens frequently when it comes to divine timing, because what happens is when we are faced with a decision that may appear to be difficult from a human perspective, or when we are faced with a decision that may be uncomfortable to us, we can be tempted to hide behind divine timing. How many times have you said, "The time just isn't right to do this," even though a deeper part of you knows this really isn't true?

I can't tell you the number of times someone tells me they are going to contact me again when the time is right, only to discover a few months later they've had to get another job, or in some cases give up their businesses entirely. Instead of making a decision to get the knowledge they need to help more people and grow their business, they chose to believe that things would get better all on their own. This is one of the most insidious lies the ego tells us: that the things around us, external to us, will get better all on their own, without us changing a thing about ourselves, or how we're doing things.

If you want your circumstances to change, you have to be willing to change.

Divine timing does not mean waiting until the exact right perfect moment to take action. It is also not an excuse for why you shouldn't do things that can support you in growing your business today. Here's what divine timing really means: in any given moment we have a choice. We can show up and choose to experience the present moment as perfect and divine, or we can choose to ignore it, wish we were somewhere else, and pretty much think the present moment sucks. Divine timing means in any moment you can make a choice to live in a way that is in alignment with your truest self, or you can choose to displace living in alignment to a future date. It really has nothing to do with when things happen, when you choose to take action, or when the right time to do something is.

Anytime is the right time, if you decide to make it so. This doesn't mean that you always get what you want, but it does mean that you begin to see every experience you encounter on your journey as offering you exactly what you need to become a more successful, abundant person. When we choose to make excuses under the guise of divine timing, we give away our power. Instead of choosing to take powerful action toward living our vision, we displace our power onto timing. "It's not my fault! I really want to do it...but the time just isn't right!"

When we choose to be powerful and make powerful decisions, we are in alignment with the idea of divine timing. When we choose to put things off, and rely on hoping and wishing, instead of being powerful, we are out of alignment with the truest of spiritual wisdom contained in the idea of divine timing. Truly understanding the nature of divine timing is what inspires the next Wealth Alignment Principle.

Wealth Alignment Principle: Don't wait until tomorrow to

take actions that can support you in creating wealth today.

I might add to this principle, don't wait until things are convenient or easy for you, to take action. What I've learned is most of the time when the timing seems inconvenient, hard, or difficult, it is exactly the time you need to take action. When things aren't working in our businesses, it's because it's something about the way we are thinking about, or relating to, our businesses that is the core problem. Taking action, even when it seems impossible, is the best way to shift, or reorient that thinking or relationship because it unlocks a level of resourcefulness inside of us that many of us may not even be aware we possess.

One of my clients is a fabulous intuitive relationship expert. Her name is Lauren Wyatt and her company is Bee Loving, Bee Wise. Lauren got so fed up with the nonsense around divine timing, that she decided to get married during the Mercury Retrograde, to show how ridiculous it is to blame the success or failure of a relationship on the time you choose to get married. She's still happily married by the way, and if you're in need of one of the best relationship coaches on the planet you can check her out at http://www.beelovingbeewise.com.

We're tempted to use the timing excuse when we aren't fully centered and grounded in our own power and resourcefulness. I'd like you to think about what might be different for you in your business if you assumed that at any given moment you had all of the resources necessary to make an empowered decision? This doesn't mean you'll say yes to every opportunity that comes your way, it simply means that whether you say yes or whether you say no, you'll start to make decisions much more quickly, because you're coming from a place of trusting yourself, rather than a place of fear.

What action or investment that you know would help you grow your business, have you been avoiding taking because you don't feel like it's the right time?

_____

_____

_____

_____

_____

_____

_____

_____

_____

_____

How would your businesses be different if you no longer said "I'll make that decision tomorrow" in any aspect of your business?

_____

_____

_____

_____

_____

_____

_____

_____

_____

_____

_____

_____

_____

Unsuccess Myth #2: The "I Don't Know How" Myth

I'm exhausted by the number of people who use terms like "practical" and "realistic" as excuses for why they can't go after their dreams. It's part of a larger cultural lie that we're collectively initiated into, which is that while we should dream big, and constantly proclaim we want more, the "more" will never really ever show up for us ordinary folk. It is part victimhood, part denial, and part ennui, and it serves to keep you safe, small and limited in your potential and capability to make a positive difference in the world.

Another expression of this is, "I really would go after my dreams if only I knew how!" Or, "If only I had the resources." Or "If only the time is right…then I really, really would!" Our next Wealth Alignment Principle deals with the approach that you take as an entrepreneur to individual obstacles and opportunities, as well as the approach you take toward manifesting and creating your perfect business vision.

Wealth Alignment Principle: How? Is the most empowering and disempowering question you can ask.

This principle may seem contradictory at first. Let's explore it in greater detail, because it really does offer a revolutionary shift in thinking. Have you ever used "how" as an excuse? I know I have. I usually cloaked it in something like, "I just don't understand how to do this." Or "I really want this, but I just don't know how to get it." It's easy to see "how" becomes incredibly disempowering when it is used as an excuse for why we can't have what we really want, or when it becomes an excuse for not taking action.

When you are more committed to the "how" you are going to get to your vision, instead of showing up every single day and saying yes to the opportunities that do present themselves, it is easy to see how it becomes incredibly paralyzing. My spiritual mentor always says, "The answer to how...is yes." Meaning instead of getting stuck on how something is going to show-up, focus instead on saying yes, and doing everything you can to take advantage of the opportunities that are right in front of you.

When how becomes a reason to stay right where you are, it is debilitating and it becomes the enemy of wealth. However, there is another way to use the how question that becomes incredibly empowering, and this is to ask the question, "How can I make this work?"

We are trained as children to make our decisions based not on what is truly possible, but on what is probable. Instead of being trained to ask, "What do I want, and how could I make it happen?" We are taught to ask, "What is practical, likely, and realistic?" If the "how" is not immediately evident, or we don't see a clear path to our dreams, we abandon them. We learn that unless we can clearly see the linkages between A, B, and C, it is most likely not worth pursuing. Why? Because it's not safe.Because we might be disappointed. Or because we don't want people to think that we are crazy dreamers.

We become trapped, rather than liberated by the how. How becomes a liberating question when we first ask, "Is this the right decision for me?" or "Is this something that I *really* want?" Asking this question first is an absolute necessity if how is to become a question that propels us forward instead of one that keeps us stuck.

The next step is to ask, "How could I make this work?" and to release our attachment to knowing everything. Asking the question, "How can I make this work?" immediately shifts you into your resourcefulness and your power. When you ask this question you'll be amazed at all of the actions and strategies you are able to come up with.

Consider an area of your business where you've been saying, "I just don't know 'how' I can do this." Instead ask, "How could I make this work?"

_____

_____

_____

_____

_____

_____

_____

_____

_____

_____

_____

_____

Often times, becoming obsessed with the how is the way we micromanage the miracle. Our focus on how something has to look or how something should look keeps us from being in gratitude about all of the amazing gifts we do have, and it can actually foreclose something better from showing up. Consider that the universe has the power to deliver something much better to you than you could ever conceive of yourself. Why? Because you are concerned with what you deserve, what you're worth, and what you're good enough to receive. The universe isn't. It operates from the principle that you are so much more than good enough. It operates from the principle that as A Course in Miracles says, "You don't ask for too much, you ask for too little."

Over and over again, in my own life and in the lives of my clients, I see how releasing our attachment to how something shows up invites the universe to work profound transformation. Our job is to show-up fully to each and every experience we are presented with, and to do our inner work. The universe will take care of the how in more amazing ways than you could ever conceive.

Unsuccess Myth #3: The "I need more information" Myth

This myth can take many forms, but at its core, it's about self-doubt. When we don't trust ourselves and the universe fully, we create stories, which then become realities, which then contribute to half-hearted action, or sometimes full on paralysis. The "I need more information" myth can take many forms, here are some examples:

- *I need more professional certifications (healing, coaching, or modality certification) before I can be successful*

- *I need more clarity before I can begin*

- *I'm waiting for a sign from the universe*

- *I'm not qualified enough to help anyone because I don't have it all figured out yet*

- *I'm not making enough money to invest in my business*

- *I'm not sure it will work*

- *I don't know how it will out*

- *I'm not sure I'm on the right path*

Are you seeing the theme of this myth? It deals with perfectionism, and the ego's lie that you always need more information, more signs from the universe, or more evidence you're on the right path before you can take any action. The strange contradiction of perfectionism is that it usually causes paralysis resulting in little or nothing getting done.

How would your business look different if, instead of waiting for yourself to feel completely ready, you took a leap of faith and started creating the infrastructure of a successful business today?

_____

_____

_____

_____

_____

_____

_____

_____

_____

_____

I learned the next Wealth Creation Principle through an intensely personal experience. When I graduated college, I had no plan for what I was going to do next in my life. I was doing one-to-one intuitive readings for people and I had an intense desire to help a lot of people through my intuitive work, but the truth is it wasn't coming together.

While I had some clients that I would help tremendously, it was on a very small scale, and I wasn't making anywhere near the impact that I knew I was capable of making. Because I had not taken the necessary action to grow my business, I found myself living in my mom's basement, and working a telemarketing job for around $8 an hour. I was sinking farther and farther into debt, and the personal emotional costs were tremendous. I experienced extreme loneliness and felt like I was failing to use the divine gifts I had been given.

Up until that point, I was always waiting for the right set of circumstances to present themselves. I would say things like, "I want to be successful, I just don't know how." This type of thinking perfectly typifies the "I need more information" myth. I thought that success would find me, or suddenly show up at my door. I falsely believed my desire to serve the world would be enough. What I've figured out is that having that desire is a critical ingredient of success, but if you don't combine that ingredient with the practical knowledge of sales and marketing no one will ever have the privilege of learning about your desire to serve.

One day I woke up, and I knew I had to do something differently. I went to my closet, packed a suitcase, quit my job without notice, called a taxi cab because I didn't even own a car at that point, and begged a friend, who lived in a nearby city, to let me stay on his couch until I could get on my feet.

It was a very dramatic move, but in that moment I was overtaken by spiritual clarity. I knew I had to be willing to commit to my vision, no matter how afraid I was. And believe me, I was afraid. I worried my family would never speak to me again. I worried the creditors would hunt me down. I worried I could potentially be homeless. I worried my friends and family would call me crazy. But in those days that followed, again and again, I heard a voice, the deep voice of truth inside of me say, "Just take the next step. If you just take the next step everything will be OK."

That is exactly what I did. I kept taking the next step, and then the next step, and then the next step. I didn't worry so much about needing to have it all figured out. I didn't worry about having all of the information to make perfect choices. Instead, I focused on putting one foot in front of the other, and doing the things that were right before me that I knew would immediately improve my life.

In a moment of crisis, like I experienced, we often feel this type of clarity because instead of worrying so much about all of those things outside of our control, we are forced to focus on only those things over which we truly do have control.

I took many actions in the next few years that contributed to me becoming successful in a very short period of time, and I'll be sharing many of those actions throughout the rest of this book, but it was this experience alone that contributed to the next Wealth Alignment Principle. A principle, I might mention, which has served me again and again. I'm often asked, "How do you get so much accomplished in such a little amount of time?" This Wealth Alignment Principle is how, because I don't waste endless amounts of energy worrying about having it all right, rather I focus on what is the next step that I need to take right now to move me closer and closer to my vision.

Wealth Alignment Principle: Success is a series of steps taken consciously and courageously. Until you take the next (or first) step the next step will not be revealed to you.

The only thing you need to be committed to is taking the next step on the journey to your vision. How often do we avoid taking action because we're waiting to have every single piece of the plan in place first?

I challenge you to never say, "I don't know" when it comes to what the next step to take in your business might be. I truly believe that while we might not know everything, we always know the next step we can take that will move us closer to success. Sometimes we have to go within to discover what this step is, which is why I believe that learning to listen to your intuition and business success go hand-in-hand.

When we allow ourselves to say, "I don't know" it takes away our agency, and energetically pushes success away from us. I like to remind myself that I always know what the next step is, whether or not I'm aware of it. Thus, if I need to uncover my next action, all I really have to do is raise my level of awareness and allow it to emerge.

Most of the time, there is a plethora of right next steps that could move us closer to our goals. Sometimes the next step is getting someone who can teach you what you need. Sometimes the next step is making a powerful investment in yourself. Sometimes the next step is calling your prior clients and reconnecting with them. Sometimes the next step is going within and planning out your next six months. Sometimes the next step is beginning to develop a new program or product. Sometimes the next step is something else entirely.

Consider one area of your business (or life) where you've been waiting for more information before you take action. How would this area of your business be transformed if you committed to taking action instead of waiting for more information?

_____

_____

_____

_____

_____

_____

_____

_____

_____

_____

_____

_____

_____

In what ways does the "I need more information myth" keep you from building the business you truly desire to own?

_____

_____

_____

_____

_____

_____

_____

_____

_____

_____

_____

_____

Moving past these Unsuccess Myths requires you to be honest with yourself about which personal myths you've created to keep success at a distance. It also requires courage, a commitment to your own personal growth and development, and a willingness to continually evaluate why you aren't taking the necessary actions to grow your business. When you are able to transcend these Unsuccess Myths you'll be amazed at how great and confident you feel. You'll also become a money and success magnet, and you'll begin to embody someone for whom wealth flows naturally and effortlessly.

CHAPTER FIVE

How to Magnetize Yourself to Clients, Money and Opportunity

I promised you at the beginning of this book I would give you profound energetic shifts necessary to transform your relationship to wealth, money, and business, and I'll continue to do so. I also promised you that I would dive into some of the very practical things you can do to grow your business. In this Chapter we're going to continue our journey of evolving our spiritual relationship to wealth, while also getting really practical about what you can do to create more clients, more money, and more opportunity.

Without clients, you don't have a business. Without money coming in every month you don't have a business. Instead, you are, as my lovely client and visionary Jan Wikman would say, "Just playing office." There's nothing wrong with this, per se, after all playing office can be *really* fun! It's great to go out into the world and tell people that you're a business owner. The problem is, it's inauthentic and makes you feel like a fraud.

The other problem is people can tell the difference between what is authentic and what is not. When you are genuinely successful, there is an energy of confidence that emanates from deep within you, and is perceived by others. When you are trying to project success you have not genuinely achieved, it actually repels clients from wanting to work with you.

Wealth Alignment Principles: Get clients first. Then build your business around those clients.

Getting clients into your business should be your number one priority when you are working to get your business off the ground. It is the single most important activity to focus on. It is more important than getting your website up, designing your logo, crafting your marketing message, worrying about your branding, becoming a master sales person, writing blogs, hanging out on social media, or any other task that you might think you need to do in order to be able to get clients.

Most entrepreneurs get it backwards. They think, "I'll get everything in place and *then* I'll go and look for some clients." Smart entrepreneurs understand until you are working with 5-10 clients consistently, you don't have the information you need to be able to do *anything* else. Without working with clients you don't know what clients *really* need. You don't know what marketing messages will actually resonate with them and get them to take action. You don't know what kind of emails, blogs, or social media posts to write. You don't have a clue about what type of branding will appeal to your audience.

There are only two things you need to begin serving clients.

1. A genuine desire to help people with whatever service or product you deliver

2. The skillset to deliver quality results

If you lack #1, close this book, email my office and we'll give you a refund. If you lack #2, that's OK, it just means you may need to get some more training so you can build your confidence. Right now you may be in the learning your craft phase, which is an exciting phase to be in, it's just not the phase in which you are ready to launch a business.

If you wait to get clients until you have a bunch of things in place, it is a colossal waste of time, energy, money, and resources. I say this because until you've worked with clients you don't really have the knowledge you need to set up your business. You're just operating from a place of what you "think" will work, or from a place of what you "think" your clients need. The result is that you end up re-doing a ton of work based on what makes sense to real people. Save yourself the trouble, and get a few clients in the beginning, and then make informed choices about how to structure and build your business using the powerful feedback of those clients.

While you can definitely survey people who are in your divine client audience, but aren't necessarily clients, it's still not going to be as powerful as actual people who pay you money giving you their feedback. When someone pays you, they feel more of a license to really tell you the truth. People who just fill out a survey might feel like they are doing you a favor, and tell you what you want to hear, even though they have no real intention of every becoming your client. Also, when you have the experience of working with clients you gain first-hand knowledge of what really gets results in a very live and real way.

The other reason why it is so essential to bring in clients, or sell your products or services in the beginning of building your business instead of waiting months and months to do so, is that there are other investments you're going to need to make in your business. You also need to make these investments quickly and decisively if you want your business to grow rapidly. It's so much easier to make these investments, whether it's in a web designer, a business coach, online ads, a physical space, a virtual assistant, etc., when you have revenue coming in. We'll talk more about which investments are the most important later on in the book, but I am a firm believer in bringing in clients and profit first, and then building the actual business structure by leveraging that profit.

If you absolutely cringe at the thought of accepting money for your services given the current state of your business, then I recommend working with a few clients on a limited basis for free. This is how my friend Heidi DeCoux, and the marketing genius behind Clear and Simple Marketing (http://www.clearsimple-marketing.com), launched her first business as a professional organizer. She asked five of her friends to become her client, and she wouldn't charge them if they agreed to do two things. First, if they were happy with her services they had to write her a glowing testimonial. Second, if they were happy with her services they had to refer her to three of their friends.

This process generated her 15 quality leads. She converted some of these leads into paying customers and her business was launched and earning money. Even in this example though, the Wealth Alignment Principle still stands. Get clients first and then build your business around those clients. It will put you miles ahead of the hang-a-shingle-and-hope-for-the-best mentality of most aspiring entrepreneurs.

Your Personal Cash Machine

I'm sure the last Wealth Alignment Principle was really scary to some of you. Maybe you thought you could wait a few weeks, or even months before going out and actually having to talk to clients. Maybe you are a perfectionist who wants to have everything just right before you put yourself out there. Maybe you are really afraid of rejection, or you worry that people will judge you if you talk to them seriously about how you can help them. If you have any of these fears coming up, that's exactly why you need to focus on bringing clients into your business, or selling your product, before you have our entire structure in place.

By the end of this Chapter, you'll know how you can begin to bring clients into your business, or sell your products and services, without having 99% of what you probably think you need to have in place, in place. Before we dive into how to actually create your Ultimate Client-Getting Plan there are two additional Wealth Alignment Principles you need to understand. Most entrepreneurs are either unaware of these principles, or integrating them into their client-getting strategy is too uncomfortable, so they do everything in their power to avoid them.

The good news is if you integrate the next two principles into your client attraction strategy, your ideal clients will be drawn to you, almost magnetically. The even better news is this principle allows you to immediately set yourself apart from everyone else in your industry, making it quick and easy, for your ideal customers to decide that yes they would love to work with you. The super-awesome-amazing news, yes there's actually more, is by choosing to implement this Wealth Alignment Principle you short-cut the need to have a perfect structure in place. This principle actually allows you to just get started taking imperfect action, which frees you from the bonds of perfectionism, centers you in your mission of service, and allows you to start cashing checks for your services while serving more people.

Wealth Alignment Principle: Your individual story is your personal cash machine.

You, by virtue of existing as a human being on this planet, have a story to tell the world. How do I know this? Because you wouldn't have even been drawn to start a business designed to help others if there wasn't something in your personal history that led you to do so. Unfortunately, we tend to discount our personal stories believing that because they weren't imparted to us as part of some formal training they are irrelevant.

I see entrepreneurs, all the time, hiding behind their resume, their credentials, or their professional experience, instead of sharing authentically, and from the heart, their life experiences. These personal experiences are so important to making you relatable to your audience. Beyond that, it creates a sense of possibility for people about what they might be able to change, shift, or transform in their own lives.

Let's say you're a weight loss coach who helps men desiring to lose 50LBS or more in a short period of time. Sharing your own personal journey around weight loss, fitness, and nutrition is going to go a long way toward people trusting you, and letting them know that the transformation is actually possible for them. If you don't share your personal story, and only focus on the amazing weight loss your clients can achieve, your potential customers will think it's great, but not accessible to them. In their minds they'll say, "That transformation sounds amazing, but I could never achieve it." When you share your personal journey with customers and clients, it shows them that the transformation they desire is not only possible, it's probable, with your help.

While your professional experience and formal training is important from the perspective of making sure you can actually deliver the results you promise, it's usually not the most important thing when someone decides whether or not to work with you. The first thing they care about is, "What are the results or benefits that you can provide them?" The second thing they care about, when making a buying decision is, "Is this someone I resonate with and/or can see myself actually working with?" By sharing your personal story, or stories, with your audience, you allow customers to experience you energetically which allows the right customers to answer that question in the affirmative.

Formal experience or training is also not the only way to become qualified to deliver services to people. I work with entrepreneurs, and I have zero academic training in business, marketing or sales. When I began my first business, doing one-to-one psychic readings for people, I didn't take any intuitive development courses or train under any famous psychic. I had a God-given ability that was meant to help people. It wasn't something anyone could give me and it would have been incredibly selfish, not to mention a huge waste of time, to wait months, or even years, before I was willing to use my gift to help others.

If you focus only on your credentials, you'll actually make yourself inaccessible to the majority of your clients by putting yourself up on an unreachable pedestal. You won't seem human to your clients, and they'll go find someone else in your industry that they feel more connected with. People don't want to work with someone who has it all together. They don't want to work with someone who is perfect. They don't want to work with someone who has never stumbled. And they certainly don't want to work with someone they feel can't empathize with where they are, and what they are struggling with.

The truth is people aren't stupid, and when you refuse to share your struggles as well as your successes it seems inauthentic. Acting like you have it all together versus sharing what you've actually lived through is the ultimate sign of insecurity, and clients can sense it from a mile away. Even if they don't consciously know why, clients will say no to working with you because something just doesn't feel right. Putting on an act, and pretending like you're something you're not, is one of the biggest ways entrepreneurs unconsciously push potential clients away.

Communicating your story, your struggles, and your experiences is one of the huge advantages that you have over mega-brands like Wal-Mart or Coca-Cola. While you may not have millions of dollars to plaster ads all over the known universe, you have something more powerful, which is your ability to individually connect with your consumers, by letting them know that you've been right where they are.

Almost every time I see a business struggling to generate enough revenue or serve clients in a way that is meaningful it is because the owner of the company has disregarded their personal story in exchange for boring and safe marketing. Or they are writing their marketing copy and presenting themselves just like every other professional in their industry. How can people pick you, out of all of the other professionals in your industry to work with, if you don't let them know about exactly what makes you different, special, and uniquely qualified to serve them? Answer: they can't.

When you open up about where you've been, in an honest way, there's also one more really big effect, which is that it provides consumers with a powerful justification for spending money with you. Right or wrong, most of us feel the need to justify spending money on things. When someone can connect genuinely to your personal story, they are able to experience a deep pull that says, "Yes, I need to invest with this person." This enables clients and customers to spend higher amounts with you, even when it may not be the most realistic thing to do.

Sharing your story isn't about splashing your energy all over the world, nor is it about sharing every single personal detail of your life with your clients. You also want to make sure that you aren't sharing your story in a way that makes your business all about you. You must remain crystal clear of the benefits that working with you, or buying your products, will produce for your clients. That said, there are several ways to frame your personal story so clients are able to relate to you, and make the decision that they would like to continue learning about your business, and eventually possibly hiring you.

I'm going to share four different ways to frame your personalized story. These certainly aren't the only ways you can share your individual life experiences with your audience, and you may choose to combine more than one of these framings.

Framing #1: Struggle to Success

The first way of framing your story is one of the most effective ways to share it with your audience. It works well if you struggled with a particular problem, and then found a way to overcome that problem, and are now experiencing a new level of success. I love this way of communicating your story to your audience because it works, regardless of what kind of business you have, and it lets your audience know that you are human.

This is the way that I choose to share my story with my audience. I was living in my mom's basement, desperately trying to grow my business, and things were just not clicking into place. Eventually I found myself cut-off from my family, living on a friend's couch, and suffocating under a mountain of debt. In just a few years, I was able to completely transform my life, achieve a new level of wealth, and more completely fulfill my mission of helping entrepreneurs achieve their vision of authentic wealth. I was struggling, and then through intense work, study, and tenacity, I stepped into success.

You also don't have to be perfect, or completely successful in order for this framing of your story to work. You may not have overcome every single obstacle yet, but as long as you've overcome a few of the obstacles your ideal client audience is struggling with, this way of framing your story will be effective.

Framing #2: Dramatic Experience Framing

Sometimes we experience a life-changing event that drastically alters the course we are on. In my first business, as a psychic medium, this was the way I chose to frame my story. Even though I had told my preschool teacher when I was just five years old, that I was a psychic, I had no plans to use my gifts to help others. I was planning on going to college and then attending law school.

At the age of 19, I lost someone incredibly close to me, my aunt Joi. This was really my first experience with death, and I didn't handle it well. I plunged into a very dark place in my life, repressed my feelings, and struggled with depression. One night, while I was alone in my dorm, my aunt appeared to me, and told me I would do readings for people all over the world, I would travel and speak, and I would do things I had never expected. At first, I thought I had lost my mind. Six months later, however, I found myself doing exactly what she had told me I would do.

In this example, you can see that I use the dramatic experience of losing a loved one to frame why I was doing intuitive readings and teaching people about psychic abilities. Choosing to use the dramatic experience framing is a great way to create emotional resonance between you and your customers. It's also relatable, because each of us has difficult experiences that we've lived through.

Framing #3: Aspirational Framing

Not all story telling requires the presence of dramatic struggle in order to be effective. Maybe you haven't lived through something traumatic, but you're still incredibly passionate about the work you do. This is where you'll want to consider focusing on something aspirational as opposed to something dramatic.

One of my clients, Jennifer Murphy of No Limits Life Coaching (http://www.nolimitslifecoach.com), was buzzing through life in a successful corporate career. She racked up promotion after promotion, and did all of the things she thought she was supposed to. Highly regarded, and having every opportunity to continue to succeed, she felt that something was missing. She started diving into personal growth and development work, exploring her own spirituality in a deeper way, and eventually got certified as a life coach. She had an aspiration to find more meaning, happiness, and fulfillment in her life. In order to achieve this desire she ultimately left her job, and launched a now-successful business coaching other busy professionals who have it all together on the outside, but want to achieve much more on the inside.

This is hardly a story of complete collapse, but that doesn't make it any less powerful to her particular target market. You'll want to consider this framing if you have customers or clients that are generally considered "already successful." Not every person is struggling desperately in their lives, but that doesn't mean they don't have particular aspirations, goals, or things they'd like to change.

Framing #4: History of Results Framing

The final way of framing your story, in most cases, will work best for those of you who have a history of serving clients, and getting results for them. In this way of telling your story, you are going to focus almost exclusively on the "social-proof" aspect of your business, by sharing your track record of quickly, and drastically, improving your clients' lives. If I were to use the history of results framing in my business, I might choose to share one particular story of success that one of my clients have experienced, but if I wanted to be even more effective I would choose to share several stories of clients who came to me when they were struggling, and have since achieved dramatic results.

Maybe you're a business coach who has helped hundreds of entrepreneurs achieve the six figure mark. Maybe you have a particular nutritional supplement that has helped thousands of people overcome depression or fatigue. One industry that this framing works particularly well in is the weight loss industry, whether you sell a supplement, offer nutritional or fitness advice, or take a more spiritual approach to weight loss, because you can provide before and after photos of your clients.

You can see how this way of sharing your story only works if you have example after example of people you've actually helped, and a compelling way of communicating that to the world. In this narrative, you are going to become the advocate or champion of the people. To complete the narrative effectively, consider sharing what first got you interested in helping others achieve such amazing transformations.

Crafting Your Story

Naturally, you can choose to combine elements from each of the framing examples I gave you above, although you'll probably have one way of telling your story that is predominant. The important thing is not that you get it exactly right the first time you tell your story, it's that you're open, honest, and share from a heart-centered place what you've been through, and why you are passionate about helping your specific clients.

It takes a lot of courage to share openly and honestly, but I know you can do it. Over time, you'll learn what elements to include, and what elements aren't all that important. You'll also learn what way of telling your story resonates best with your particular audience. If you'd like, experiment with framing your story in a couple of different ways and ask your friends, family, or customers which way they find the most compelling.

However you choose to frame your story, it must not only humanize you, it must also provide a justification for why you are qualified to do the work you do. It should establish in your customers' minds that there is something special about you, and that you have a very clear reason to be supporting them in their personal growth or transformation. Even if you don't deal in what we typically would consider "transformational work" you still need to share your story, because it sets you apart from others in your industry, and creates an understanding of why a person would want to engage with your business.

Now it's time to compose your personal story in a way that you would feel good (not comfortable) about communicating it to your audience. Take a few deep breaths, because sometimes this can bring up some emotional stuff, and then take several minutes to write out your personal story. If you've been in business for a while, you may have forgotten or lost touch with this story, and reconnecting with it will often produce an income and client breakthrough. If you're new to business, this may be your first time connecting the dots between your personal experience and your mission in your business. Good luck!

Choose one or more of the Story Framings above and write out your personal story.

_____

_____

_____

_____

_____

Now, I want you to choose how you will share this story with your ideal client audience. Will you make a "Welcome Video" for your website, send out a snail mail letter, share it in a blog or eZine article, or possibly even do a live call for your audience. Whatever way you choose, just make sure that you openly and honestly share your story about how you got to where you are, and why you care about helping people.

Too often we have breakthroughs, but refuse to ground them in practical action, by making commitments, setting goals and establishing deadlines. I'm asking you *not* to do that by making a commitment to share this important story with your tribe. Ready to commit?

I will share my personal story with my audience by _____, and I will commit to doing so by (date) _____.

In the next Chapter we'll be covering exactly how you can create a plan to begin to bring new clients into your business. Armed with the understanding that you *must* enroll clients in order to have a functioning business, and your personal story, you are now in a much better position to select marketing strategies that will actually be effective for your business.

CHAPTER SIX

Constructing Your Ultimate Client-Getting Plan

You'll notice this book is much different from most of the marketing volumes you've consumed. That is a very conscious choice on my part, because even though there's a part of us that screams, "Just tell me what to do, and I'll do it," formulas, marketing tactics, and sales strategies that are chosen unconsciously, meaning without thinking through how you relate to these different formulas, tactics, and strategies, simply won't be effective. This is why two people can implement the exact same strategies in their businesses and get radically different results.

In this Chapter, I am going to show you how to get connected to your divine spiritual gifts, and then use that awareness to select marketing strategies that will get you results for your business. If you've gotten this far in the book, you've done some major personal and spiritual work, and you're now ready to create what I call the Ultimate Client-Getting Plan. This plan will be your roadmap to more clients, more money, and more satisfaction. Even with this plan, there will be times when you have to improvise, be flexible, and make snap decisions to grow your business and consistently up level your revenue.

Wealth Alignment Principle: Consciously designed and consistently implemented plans yield big results.

This client attraction plan only works when you have the right structure to actually support clients, which includes a well-thought-out six figure business structure, a way for clients to work with you long-term or to invest again and again with your company, and a genuine desire to solve specific problems and help people make specific improvements in their lives. Luckily, if you've been doing the work, you're well on your way to having that structure in place.

Step #1: Identify Your Divine Gifts, Talents, and Strengths

Most people don't choose marketing strategies that work because they choose them independent of their personalities. How different would the results you get in your marketing be if instead of randomly choosing tactic after tactic to try, otherwise known as "desperation marketing," you consciously took the time to select marketing strategies that worked with your spiritual gifts?

Do you even know what your divine gifts are? Of course you do! You may call them your natural talents or abilities, or the things that just come naturally to you, but these are actually your divine gifts, given to you from the universe to help you create a thriving and monetized business. Think of all of the things you do well that seem like no big deal to you because they come so naturally and easily to you.

Wealth Alignment Principle: The things that come most easily to you often hold the most money making potential...because they don't come easily to others.

This Wealth Alignment Principle is not meant to imply that you don't have to work to perfect your craft, or strive to become better at selling your services, or stop improving your products; what it does mean, is most often what comes easily and naturally to you is extremely valuable because it doesn't come naturally and easily to others. Two of my divine talents are charisma and communication. Networking, connecting, and sharing my story with people through words comes very naturally to me, and because it comes so easily, it's easy for me to discount it and to treat it like it's insignificant. If I treat those divine gifts like that, not only do I lose, but my clients lose out as well, because learning how to effectively communicate and how to tap into their inner charisma could be a complete game-changer for them!

If I chose to not share my divine gifts, other entrepreneurs will not learn how to harness the power of communication and charisma that comes so naturally to me. Maybe you are someone people naturally feel safe around. This is one of your divine gifts and you can harness it in your branding, your marketing, and potentially even in the services you offer. A feeling of safety is a great quality to have if you're an accountant, financial planner, or you deal with people's money in some way, because people need to feel safe with where they are putting their money.

Maybe you're a person who sees connections other people tend to miss. You might be a great career coach, helping someone plan out their career path and get results by seeing the moves they need to take before they do. Or, maybe you have always been a fantastic student, able to retain a lot of information, so you may have a position as a consultant who can synthesize large amounts of information and present them to your clients. Maybe you have a great sense of humor, and the ability to remain comfortable in most situations, so helping people with their dating lives may be the perfect fit for you.

Are you getting the picture? All of the things that you rock at, and have always been good at, hold the key to unlocking your wealth and success potential. I'm not going to give you a list of your divine gifts because I believe that we are all blessed with so many different talents and abilities. I feel like if I give you a list, I may be foreclosing your ability to identify one of your own divine gifts. What I am going to do is walk you through a short exercise to get you to discover your divine gifts.

What are you good at?

_____

_____

_____

_____

_____

_____

_____

What do you love doing?

_____

_____

_____

_____

_____

_____

What comes easily and naturally to you?

_____

_____

_____

_____

_____

_____

_____

What innate qualities are you the most likely to discount in yourself?

_____

_____

_____

_____

_____

_____

My divine gifts are...

_____

_____

_____

_____

_____

_____

_____

_____

Take a moment to breathe and absorb what you just walked your-self through. For some of you, this is going to be a major break-through moment because you'll become aware of how you've been selling yourself short for most of your life. When I uncovered my divine gifts and abilities, I realized that is exactly what I had been doing, but I also felt an enormous sense of relief because I could finally stop pretending to be someone I'm not and doing things that weren't authentic to who I was.

That is the power of understanding your divine gifts. You get to build a business, and choose marketing strategies, that are aligned to those gifts. Up until this point, you may have been doing things because you think it's what you're supposed to do, or because you saw other entrepreneurs doing those things. Now, you get to take the next step in creating your Ultimate Client Getting Plan in alignment and pressure-free.

I believe that everything gets easier when you work on both the vibrational and human levels. Our natural impulse is to either work exclusively in the realm of what is "realistic," or to ignore reality completely and keep our heads stuck in the clouds. When you are able to use the energy of possibility and potential, what you might think of as "high-vibrating" energy, and then ground that energy into taking actual human action, you begin to get the results you truly desire, and as a bonus experience, a much higher level of satisfaction and meaning while taking those actions.

Getting in touch with our unique spiritual gifts, and choosing client attraction and marketing strategies that compliment those gifts, is one of the most powerful ways to integrate the spiritual and practical realm to yield big results.

Step #2: Setting Your Client Goals

We have one more step to go before we get into actually selecting the strategies that will make up your Ultimate Client Getting Plan, and that is to set goals around how many clients you actually need to get to make the income you want. I believe strongly in knowing how many clients you need to bring in each month, how many clients you typically enroll in a month, and through what activities you get those clients. Let's do a simple exercise to map-out your income goals and client numbers.

As you map out these numbers, I invite you to stretch yourself a little while also choosing a number that feels realistic and possible to you. If you choose something that feels unattainable, the universe will accept the unattainability as true, and you won't be able to achieve it. Instead, choose a number that would feel great to make, but that actually seems possible to you. For some of you, that number may only be around $1,000 a month right now, and that's perfectly fine. For some of you, it may be doubling your income. I mention this because too often people want to go from a very low number to a very high number, and while this is certainly possible, I believe it's better and more effective, to stair step your way up the income staircase.

When we choose a number that doesn't seem possible for us to make, it's actually a way of hiding out. Let me explain what I mean. When we choose numbers we don't believe we can actually earn, it displaces our responsibility to go out and make that money onto the universe. It's a form of denial by which we say, "Well I put this number out there, so now it's the universe's job to give it to me." Wrong! It's the universe's job to create the situations and opportunities, it's your job to go out and actually create the revenue. I began by charging $15 for a 30 minute reading, and then slowly raised my prices to where they are now. In the beginning, $15 was what I needed to charge to gain confidence, but what I did was continue to raise my prices over and over again as I knew the value of what I provided was higher.

With all of that in mind, let's go through a short exercise to figure out your income goals and client numbers so that we can select marketing strategies that will help you achieve those goals.

How much money would you like to make this month (a realistic stretch)? $_____

How many new clients do you need to bring in this month to meet those numbers? _____

For example, if you wrote down $5,000 and you have a package that you sell for $1,000 then you need to bring in 5 new clients this month, assuming you're starting at zero in terms of revenue. If you wrote down $5,000, and you already have signed up one client for $1,000, then you need to sign up 4 more clients to meet your goals.

This is where, for some of you, selling high-ticket is going to make your job a lot easier. Unless you're selling a widget of some kind, if you need to bring in over 20 clients a month, you probably have a nearly impossible task in the beginning. When you're not a known commodity it's much easier to focus on bringing in a few higher paying, quality clients that will give you referrals, happily write testimonials, and tell all of their friends about you. All this means is you need to raise your prices or develop a package that you can sell at a higher rate.

It's much easier, yes, you read that right, to sell longer-term packages, at higher prices, than shorter-term packages at lower prices, because the perceived and actual value is infinitely higher. It also seems more real and authentic to people that they could really get the transformation they want over a longer period of time, which makes it seem like a safe, and more reasonable, investment. Not to mention these clients will get the best results, turning them into happy and loyal customers who are excited to recommend you to others.

If you do sell a product, you can still use all of these strategies, but you will also need to invest some money in leveraged strategies (like pay-per-click or traditional advertising) to drive traffic and get sales because your one-to-one selling time is going to max out quickly.

If you're tempted to skip over this step...don't! If you aren't courageous enough to put clarity to your numbers and specifically identify your client and income goals, then how in the heck are you going to be courageous enough to actually enroll clients? When we find a way to get specific about what we want to accomplish, we not only take ourselves seriously as entrepreneurs, but we begin to set the wheels, of universal law, in motion that make the delivery of those clients infinitely more likely.

Step #3: Selecting Your Marketing Strategies

What is opening up for your right now? Just take a moment to observe how you feel in your body. Are you excited? Nervous? Uncomfortable? Ready to keep moving? Some combination? If you've worked through the first two steps, you've already set yourself up for success because you know exactly what you are amazingly good at (it may not have been what you thought), and you know exactly the number of clients you need to bring in this month to meet a powerful income goal.

There are entrepreneur's that play office for the entire lifespan of their business, and never know either of these two things. You do, which shows me that you are serious about going from an entrepreneur who just plays office, to an empowered entrepreneur who makes great money and actively builds wealth each day in their business.

Step #3 is where we're actually going to pick your marketing tactics. Your marketing tactics are the particular activities you engage in to enroll clients. All of these marketing tactics together, consistently implemented, are what we'll call your Marketing Strategy. It's important to pick a powerful combination of tactics so that your overall strategy yields results.

There are so many different ways to market your business, and I'm going to give you a far from comprehensive list here, but what I am going to do is break down several marketing strategies for you to choose from. I also make a recommendation for how many of them you should choose. The best combination of marketing is going to include some online, and some offline, components.

As you read through this list, make a cursory note of which marketing strategies seem the most in alignment with your divine gifts. If you love speaking and connecting to big groups of people, public speaking and networking will be fantastic choices. If you're more introverted, you may choose to write articles and nurture referrals. It is important to choose the strategies that resonate with who you are, instead of choosing strategies based on what you think you should do.

My director of operations Valerie Weber, and CEO of Griffin Executive Virtual Assistants, built her successful practice in just a matter of months entirely through referrals. She is much more introverted, so speaking from stage or networking at large gatherings would not have been true to her, and beyond that, it wouldn't have been true to her brand, which is really built around quietly doing the hard work so you don't have to.

You'll notice that I give you guidelines for exactly how many marketing strategies you should choose from each of the following categories. While you are welcome to choose more, I really feel that these guidelines will give you enough to work on. It's important to understand these strategies each need cultivation and consistent attention, so it's better to choose fewer strategies, and to go into greater depth and consistent implementation with each strategy, rather than spread yourself so thin that you are unable to put any of them into practice fully.

You'll also notice that I only recommend beginning with one social media strategy. Social media, for most entrepreneurs in the beginning, is a huge waste of time. When you choose to focus on a singular platform you can get to know it very well and make tweaks to get better and better results. When I was growing my business I chose to focus on LinkedIn. You can head over to http://www.con-sciousguidebookgifts.com if you're interested in a video training on how I was able to generate five figure months using LinkedIn.

As you gain more comfort, and begin to systematize your efforts, you can add additional strategies to your marketing calendar. Review the following marketing tactics and list out which ones you will integrate into your Ultimate Client Getting Plan.

Quick-Start Marketing (Select At Least Three)
Networking
Referrals
Public Speaking
Sponsorships
Attending live events
Simple PR (get interviewed by others)

Online Marketing (Select One in Addition to Email Marketing)
Email marketing (required)
Blogging
Video (YouTube)
Webinars/Teleclasses
Article Writing

Social Media Marketing (Select One)
Facebook
Twitter
LinkedIn
Pinterest

Paid Marketing (Optional)
Pay-per-click ads
Print advertising
Paid PR

Marketing Must-Haves (Required)
Follow-up with old prospects
Client upsells

Advanced Marketing
If you're making under $50,000 per year don't choose any at this time. Over $50,000 choose one.
Joint venture partnerships
2-day live event (hosted by you)
Telesummit
Online joint venture giveaway
Kindle book or other online book launch

Choosing strategies that work with your strengths does not mean you should only choose strategies with which you are completely comfortable. You must be willing to stretch, grow, and try things outside of your comfort zone. I recommend choosing at least one marketing strategy you know is going to challenge you and contribute to your personal growth. The dividends are often amazing.

How do you feel right now? Hopefully empowered, because you have just given yourself a powerful structure that is going to support you in serving more people. If you have questions about how to implement any of these strategies, it might be a great idea to request an Intuitive Business Breakthrough Session with one of my team members. They can help you figure out a step-by-step way to customize the above strategies to your specific business needs, and make recommendations about what resources you will need to be able to utilize any of these tactics to maximize results.

You can request a session here

http://www.goo.gl/xMW1kx

What I love about selecting your marketing tactics, and combining them into your plan, is that it is a very powerful way of grounding your vision, which can sometimes feel squishy and far away, into very practical human action. As you can tell, I am a firm believer that spiritual vision combined with practical action produces fantastic results, and by working through this step, that's exactly what you've done. It can be tempting to stay in our minds, in our imaginations, and in our dreams about what we want to create. While it's powerful to vision in that way, it's even more powerful when we funnel our vision into specific and grounded action.

Step #4: Drafting Your Plan

You know your gifts, you've set your goals, and you've selected various marketing activities, which I have to say if you haven't celebrated yourself already, please do. This is a huge amount of progress, and now it's time to take that progress and actually put it into a working plan.

The best way I know to begin drafting this plan is by using a calendar. I recommend Google Calendar, but there are many online and offline options. I like online because it's easy to track, is connected to your smart phone, and will allow you to send calendar invitations to potential clients. Offline can also work well and is great for giving you a large visual of what your coming months look like.

After you've determined what calendar solution you will use, you are going to want to add all of the marketing tactics to the calendar. Decide which strategies you will implement daily, which strategies you will implement monthly, and so on.

Some daily client attraction activities include: reaching out to potential clients, following-up with prospects, social media marketing, and connecting with new people. Not all activities need to be done every single day, some can be done weekly. Great weekly client attraction activities include: asking for referrals (can also be monthly), attending a networking event, reaching out to potential JV partners, article writing, blogging, and sending out a weekly email.

There are also some activities that you will want to do once a month. Monthly client attraction activities can include: networking, attending live events, public speaking, teleseminars, webinars, doing JV interviews, writing a guest blog post, asking for referrals, or running a paid ad campaign. You may also have some activities that are quarterly and yearly, and you'll also want to add those to your calendar as needed.

One question I get asked a lot is how much should I be marketing every single day. If you have a few clients right now, but you really need to bring in more clients and increase your revenue, I would recommend marketing at least 4 hours each day. If you have yet to bring in any clients, or you are really struggling financially, then you probably need to market an additional 1-2 hours. We'll talk about what you should be marketing in a moment, because you don't just market "your business," but I'm guessing that you've been spending way to little time marketing.

There's also a difference between marketing tactics that are going to build credibility and bring in clients over time, like PR, and marketing tactics that have a much quicker effect on your bank account, like having a conversation with someone at a networking event or as a result of a referral. If you want to build sustainable profit, and ultimately wealth, you need a combination of both.

Here's an example of what your Ultimate Client Getting Plan may look like. This example is actually very similar to my initial Ultimate Client Getting Plan that took me from roller coastering every single month to consistent profitable months.

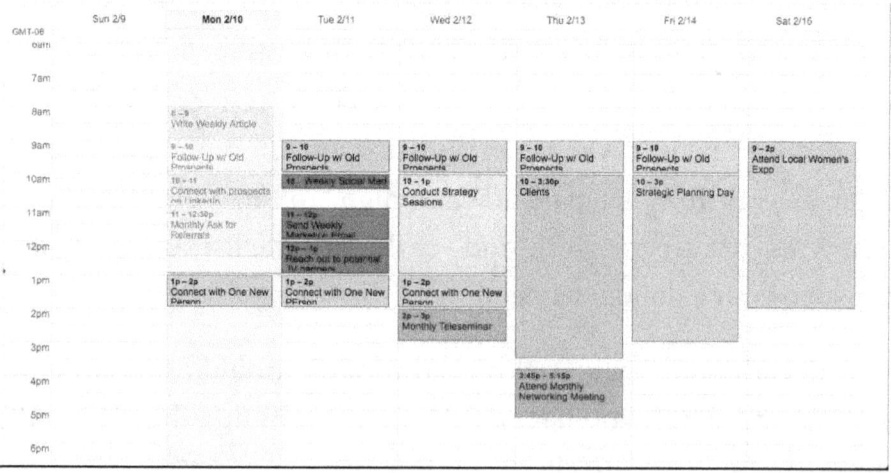

Now that you've built this plan, I want you to take a few minutes to look it over, and evaluate your lead triggers or activities that directly bring new leads into your business. Do you have activities every single week designed to bring new leads into your world? If not, it means that you chose strategies that felt safe and comfortable to you, so you'll need to go back and redo Step #3. If you do, congratulations, you should be proud of yourself.

I also want you to look over this plan, take a breath, and really understand what it represents. It doesn't represent words on a page, it represents you taking courageous action that will actually allow you to serve more people and make a bigger impact in your business. Remember this when you have a hard day, or when you don't feel like implementing them. Overtime you'll learn which tactics work extremely well, and which tactics you need to tweak or modify because they aren't getting you the results you desire.

Step #5: Your Sacred Commitment to Clients

You now have a plan that can take you to unparalleled levels of wealth and success. Most coaches and consultants would simply leave you there, but I noticed that just having the plan, even a really good plan, is not enough for most conscious entrepreneurs. We are sensitive, and tend to absorb a lot of excess energy, and so our ability to get overwhelmed, to be distracted, or to stop and start in our marketing is exceptionally high. That is why I decided to add a fifth step to the process of creating your Ultimate Client Getting Plan.

This step involves making a sacred commitment to yourself, the universe, and your clients, to implement the plan you have just invested serious energy in creating. I believe sticking to this plan really is a sacred commitment because, whether or not people get to experience your business, depends on whether or not you implement this plan. Whether or not people get the help you provide with your services or the benefit of your products depends on whether or not, regardless of what else is happening your life, you take action on this plan. With every conscious action we take, we renew our commitment to actually serving people in the world.

Take a deep breath and say the following:

I ask for the support I need from the universe and my highest self in implementing my Ultimate Client Getting Plan. May the forces of good conspire to help me recognize and create opportunities, and may I become the person I need to become in order to create unparalleled levels of wealth in my business through all I do.

Feel the vibration, and the power in those words, and know as you say them you are giving yourself permission to welcome in new levels of wealth and abundance into your business and into your life. Congratulations, you've just made a commitment, of which, the benefits will ripple through the world.

I know that this Chapter might have made some of you uncomfortable because we dove into the specifics of what it takes to run a successful business. Many times, people love when I talk about wealth, abundance, and manifesting, but get uncomfortable when we talk about how to put it into action because, when we take inspired action, we see all of the places we have to grow and improve to be able to get what we want, and frankly, it doesn't always feel great. If you are strong enough to move through it, give yourself the space to process those feelings and take action anyway, your business becomes a wealth producing force for good. Anyone can focus on manifesting or imagining, but it is the rare person who can utilize those techniques while grounding them in the necessary action. If you've completed this Chapter, you are one of those rare individuals, and I honor you.

CHAPTER SEVEN

Writing Your New Wealth Story

To say most of us have a complicated relationship with money and wealth is to severely understate the issue. In fact, when it comes to making more money and creating more wealth in our lives, one of the first things we must accept is that we have much to unlearn when it comes to what we hold true about money and success. Over and over again, as I create more revenue in my business and construct a life that feels wealthy to me in all ways, and on all levels, I realize it's almost always a process of letting go of what I previously believed to be true, and replacing the false beliefs with a new set of assumptions and understandings that are more in line with what I really want to create.

It is so important to continually evaluate our assumptions about money and wealth because it these assumptions, both conscious and unconscious, that determine the entirety of what we see around us. Even though we often think of our thoughts as distinct from our actions, they are inextricably linked. What starts out as an unconscious belief, becomes a conscious emotion, and quickly starts to have an impact on the decisions and choices we make.

If you happen to be reading this book, you probably already believe our thoughts and emotions create our reality. I tend to attract advanced spiritual thinkers, but even if you aren't convinced yet, that's no problem, we'll explore the connection between our emotions and beliefs around money and how they have real consequences for how you run your business.

Your Money Beliefs Dictate Your Money Reality

I asked my client Janet Tyler Johnson, certified financial planner and founder of Corporate Hostage No More, to explain how the thoughts, attitudes, and beliefs we have around money affect us in very practical ways. I'm going to share with you what she wrote here, so that you can really get clear on how our early experience with money has everything to do with the way we run, manage, and grow our businesses.

"When it comes to money, many of us carry around both conscious and sub-conscious beliefs that are fear-based, making it difficult to have an abundant (high vibrating) relationship with it. Until we uncover these beliefs, and come from a higher vibrating place with money, it is very difficult, and often impossible, to stop struggling with money and/or attract greater amounts of money into our lives.

Let me give you some examples. You may think you have only positive beliefs around money, but as a child, your parents fought about money all the time and you took on the unconscious belief that money creates conflict, therefore, if there's no money in your life there will be no conflict.

Or, in my case, I was a very picky eater when I was a child so my parents created the "clean plate club." If I finished everything on my plate, they would put a few coins into a glass jar. It wasn't until decades later, when talking about beliefs around money with a colleague, that I shared this story and he heard that I had gotten paid to do something I didn't want to do. That was a huge "aha" moment for me as I realized that I always felt I was entitled to more money when doing something I didn't want to do, but when doing something I loved, I didn't care if I got paid or not. That could be a huge problem when running a business, especially a business where I spend my days doing only what I love to do.

We all have these unconscious beliefs around money that often require help in uncovering. One question that can help you begin to uncover your own beliefs around money is this: What is your first memory of money? What is the first thing that comes up for you when you ask yourself that question?

For many people I have worked with, this one question led to a big "aha" moment. Does it for you?

If unconsciously, or consciously, we have fears around money, or beliefs that are fear-based such as shame, guilt, anger, remorse, scarcity thinking, or feeling we don't deserve more money, or that money is evil, or only evil people have great abundance, our money frequency is low.

In order to raise your own money frequency, you need to uncover the beliefs that are not serving you and develop a loving relationship with money. Money can do great things for us. No, it can't necessarily create happiness in our lives, but it can make our lives, and the lives of others, easier. Money, in itself, is a neutral thing. It can be used for good or evil, but we have to start believing it can do great good if we want more of it.

I often think of the change I could make in the world if I won the lottery. I wouldn't be out yacht shopping, although I have a pretty cool house with a built-in pool picked out, but I would use that money as a force for good.

There is nothing wrong with having a lot of money, in fact, it is your divine right to live a life filled with abundance. If you truly want to raise your own money frequency, seek out a coach or mentor or healer who can help you uncover your subconscious beliefs and shift your relationship with money for good. And begin living your life from a high-vibration place, a place of gratitude, appreciation, love and joy. If you can do that, your money problems are over!"

Learn more about Janet at http://www.janettylerjohnson.com, *and she's been generous to offer you her Corporate Escape Plan report as a free bonus. Thanks Janet!*

Nowhere is the connection between thoughts and reality clearer than when we look at our relationship to money, and the financial circumstances we have created for ourselves. Think about what you were told about money as a child. Were you told that making too much money makes a person greedy? Maybe a parent modeled the behavior of working all the time, in return they made great money, but for you, as a child, you drew a connection between sacrifice and money. Or maybe you grew up with great affluence, and making money has always come naturally for you.

I'm guessing, unless you've done a lot of personal work around wealth, money, and success, that whatever messages, both implicit and explicit that you internalized as a child, are creepily similar to what you see currently reflected in your life. I grew up with two parents who worked incredibly hard and struggled to keep providing for my siblings and me. Money was something that you had to work very hard for, and even then there was rarely ever a surplus of it. The world seemed like a very cruel place in which there simply wasn't enough to go around.

This was exactly the reality that I created for myself as an adult. Even though I was incredibly bright, talented, and tenacious, everything I did felt really hard to me. I was always struggling, never making enough money, and the money I did make, I was incredibly fearful that it would all go away. I now know it felt that way because it was the level of consciousness I had been initiated into. I literally thought that reality into existence. In order to create a new reality for myself, a reality which reflected the level of wealth I desired, I had to deconstruct the beliefs and assumptions that were very true to me at this level of consciousness, and replace them with new, more positive and affirming beliefs. It's the new set of assumptions I'm going to share with you here.

It's easy to see the habits of our parents we've adopted, but it isn't always that we accept the beliefs we were raised with, sometimes we do the opposite and rebel against their way of doing things. This is why you may have a very dysfunctional relationship to money, you embraced certain parts of your family's thinking while rebelling against other parts. A deep confusion around money results from this. I'll give you an example: my mom was very financially responsible when it came to always making sure her family was taken care of, and because of this, I really noticed that she struggled and had to give up a lot of things for herself.

I came to associate the idea of being financially responsible with the idea of sacrifice and living a difficult life. Unconsciously I rebelled against this association, and in my early twenties created a lot of credit card debt from frivolous and unnecessary spending. I wanted to have a fun life where I was provided for, but instead of doing it in a healthy way, I did it in a completely unhealthy way. I could have learned a great lesson from my mom, but instead I chose rebellion because my childhood mind drew connections and associations that a child's mind would draw. As an adult, I had to evaluate these assumptions and step firmly into my power to make a new choice: I can be financially responsible without having to struggle, sacrifice, or give things up.

Sometimes this part of the work can be very painful because it requires us to look at some of the things we dealt with growing-up. This is not about blaming your parents or anyone else. They were doing their personal spiritual work as well, and it's important to acknowledge all of the good things they did for us, and all of the gifts they gave us, as well as looking at what we need to let go of so that we can form a healthier relationship to money.

We must also take one hundred percent responsibility for our emotions, decisions, thoughts, beliefs, and of course actions. Even though our thinking was formed as children, we have made the decisions as adults to buy into some, or all, of that mistaken thinking, and if we take this work to a place of blame and judgment, instead of a place of forgiveness and understanding, we won't be in the best place to create wealth and run successful businesses.

It can also be easy to simply avoid this Chapter because it's uncomfortable, or to slip into denial by saying, "Yep, I've got that handled. I've already dealt with that." If you don't have the level of success or wealth that you desire, then the reality is you still have unconscious, and conscious, beliefs that are holding you back. If you were one hundred percent in abundance consciousness, you would have exactly the level of wealth you desired at any given moment. Approach the work with an open mind by being willing to look at where you're uncomfortable, where you've made choices based on outmoded assumptions, and where you can integrate a new way of thinking into your life and business.

Out With the Old...In With the New

It's time to begin writing your new money and wealth story. Achieving new levels of wealth involves brining a deep level of awareness to what is not working and why, and then replacing the broken thinking with a new, more evolved way of understanding our lives. That is why creating authentic wealth in every area of your life isn't just about pushing yourself incredibly hard to make money, it's about adopting a holistic view of abundance, which includes, but is not limited to, your bank account.

Let's begin the work of looking at some assumptions you may have about money. For each old, limiting belief, I also give you a new, powerful Wealth Alignment Principle. In order to get the most out of this section, pay attention to how you feel in your body as you read through each old assumption and new belief. You're looking for places where you feel uncomfortable or you experience resistance. The places where you feel the most discomfort are the places where you'll need to do the most work, which also means there is the most opportunity for growth and breakthrough.

As we go through, I'll be asking you to rate each old assumption in terms of how true it feels to you. Then, I'll ask you where this problem behavior is showing up in your business. For instance, the first assumption deals with the belief that making great money only occurs after years of struggle. If you are constantly struggling in three or four major areas in your business, even though you're great at the work you do, this old assumption is showing up in those three or four areas. If you hold the belief that only bad people make great money, you may be tempted to discount or give away your services.

Finally, I'll introduce the new Wealth Alignment Principle and give you an opportunity to write a new wealth story with this Wealth Alignment Principle in mind. Are you ready to write your new wealth story?

Old assumption: Making great money only occurs after years of struggle.

How true does this feel to you?

1 2 3 4 5 6 7 8 9 10

Where in your business is this showing up? How is this belief sabotaging your wealth creation ability?

_____

_____

_____

_____

_____

_____

_____

Wealth Alignment Principle: Making great money can happen quickly when you take courageous and inspired action.

Struggle is a human construction, not a spiritual reality. You can make money as quickly as you are truly ready to take aligned action to get it, and put yourself in a spiritual place to be able to receive it. Most of us have struggled a lot, and if you've worked through the framing of your story exercises, you can see how those struggles are actually some of the best lessons we've had when it comes to being able to help others. We must remove the psychic trauma of our struggles, so that they become lessons and ways to help others, instead of wounds that paralyze us from moving forward.

Most of us don't feel worthy of receiving money or we saw a model of making money that looked hard and required a lot of struggle. We buy into the idea that only when we have struggled enough, suffered enough, bled and sweated enough, can we have what we need.

When we hold this idea, either consciously or unconsciously, we are actually flipping the universal switch to suffering and struggle. We say, "This has to be hard," and the universe responds by accepting that as true and replicating suffering and struggle in our lives and in our businesses. If you want to create money quickly and easily, you've got to begin by flipping the switch, and then consciously take action until that becomes your reality.

What is your new wealth story around struggle and money in your business, and in your life, moving forward?

_____

_____

_____

_____

_____

_____

_____

_____

_____

_____

_____

_____

_____

_____

Old assumption: The only way to make great money is by working all the time and sacrificing the other things in my life that are important to me.

How true does this feel to you?

1 2 3 4 5 6 7 8 9 10

Where in your business is this showing up? How is this belief sabotaging your wealth creation ability?

_____

_____

_____

_____

_____

_____

_____

_____

_____

_____

_____

_____

_____

Wealth Alignment Principle: It's possible to work less while creating more wealth than you ever thought possible.

I often see this showing up with people whose parents were workaholics, or parents of children who really want to be good parents and worry that they will sacrifice too much time with their kids if they were running a successful enterprise. It's not a completely illegitimate fear because there are ways to set-up your business where all you do is push, push, push until you make a certain amount of money. Ultimately, this isn't sustainable either for your health, your emotional or mental wellbeing, or for your bank account. I've seen entrepreneur's burn themselves into the ground because they work in this mode 24/7.

Fortunately, there are also many ways to build your business in a way that takes into account the kind of lifestyle you want to have. For example, I usually take Friday's off to start my weekend early, take a trip every couple of months for my own leisure and to spend time with my husband, and I can easily build more vacation time into my schedule anytime I want without my income suffering. I also take time every day to walk our dog and listen to music which is my way of getting exercise and keeping myself mentally clear.

Part of being a conscious entrepreneur means you don't just want to have a business to make great money, you also want to live a lifestyle that fills you up on all levels. There's no point in building a business where you're going to treat yourself like a poorly accommodated employee. You can build your business to take into account the kind of lifestyle you want to have, including how much time you want to work and how much time you don't, and create a business around those needs.

As you make more money, you can also outsource a huge amount of your work, for a very low investment. Whether it's someone to buy your groceries, or a virtual assistant to help with administration and basic technological tasks, as you build wealth, you can build your team, giving you the option to work less while getting paid more.

What would your life look like if you were able to work less while getting paid more?

_____

_____

_____

_____

_____

_____

_____

_____

_____

_____

_____

_____

Old assumption: People who need my services won't be willing to pay great money for them. Or, people can't afford to pay for my services.

How true does this feel to you?

1 2 3 4 5 6 7 8 9 10

Where in your business is this showing up? How is this belief sabotaging your wealth creation ability?

_____

_____

_____

_____

_____

_____

_____

_____

_____

Wealth Alignment Principle: When we value ourselves and our work,

we easily convey that value, and the right customers are happy to

pay great prices.

Where in your life are you not finding a way to invest in what you need? In my experience, when people have issues about charging high prices, it's usually because they've created a story in their own lives about what they can or can't afford. We tend to attract in our clients the behavior and attitudes we are exhibiting. What if it were possible you could find the resources for anything that was truly important to you? This is a powerful and wealthy awareness, which some people will never access. It doesn't make them bad people, it just means we all have a choice about how we view our finances and our bank accounts. Whether you choose to believe your story, or whether you choose to do whatever it takes, no excuses, to find a way, is completely up to you.

It's also important to understand there is no limit to what people are willing to pay for value. When you package your services or your products in a way that is full of value, it becomes easy for customers to say yes to you. When I develop my products, services, or packages I have a test that I apply. Would someone get at least ten times the transformation compared to the investment? If the answer is no, I add more value until I feel intuitively I've met the test. That way when I'm speaking with a client, in my mind and in my heart, I feel like it's a complete no-brainer for them to say yes to working with me.

When you talk about the results a customer or client will receive from working with you, or purchasing your products, you immediately shift the tone of the conversation. You go from trying to convince someone of the value, to creating a space where the customer automatically desires what you have, and the conversation is simply around whether or not they will find a way to make it work. Sometimes we forget to talk about the results and instead talk about the logistics or modality related to our services and products. Anytime we're talking about process, instead of value and results, customers are likely to walk away instead of purchasing.

As conscious entrepreneurs, it is incredibly easy to discount our products, programs, and services because we feel sorry for people or because we aren't confident of standing in our own value. In my experience, the clients that I've discounted my rates for have been some of the least committed clients I've ever worked with. Further, they simply aren't in the resourceful and creative place necessary to achieve long-term, lasting transformations in their lives.

For so long, I lived in fear of people saying no to me. I felt like if someone said no to my services or came up with an excuse or story about why it wasn't the right time, they couldn't afford it, or they needed to take some time to think about, they were personally rejecting me or making a statement about my personal value.

Now I understand it actually has nothing to do with me, it's their own fear of succeeding or actually getting what they want. Instead of degrading my value by reducing my prices, I choose to speak powerfully about the results that a client will receive from working with me, and participating actively, and I help them find a way to do something they need.

What would be different in your business and your life if you stood fully in your value, and knew with complete confidence, that someone absolutely needed your services?

_____

_____

_____

_____

_____

_____

_____

_____

_____

_____

_____

_____

_____

Old assumption: If I become wealthy everyone will want something from me. Or, people will only like me for my wealth.

How true does this feel to you?

1 2 3 4 5 6 7 8 9 10

Where in your business is this showing up? How is this belief sabotaging your wealth creation ability?

_____

_____

_____

_____

_____

_____

_____

_____

_____

_____

_____

_____

_____

_____

Wealth Alignment Principle: **Achieving authentic wealth requires healthy boundaries, which means you'll have more to give in an appropriate way, and you'll be comfortable saying no to giving in inappropriate ways.**

This Wealth Alignment Principle is a little bit more confusing than any other principle in the book, and yet I still think it's incredibly important. If you just want to make money, there are a million shortcuts, unethical ways, and scammy practices you can engage in to make a quick dollar. It won't be sustainable, it will make you feel terrible, and it won't result in fulfillment, which is why I don't consider just making a few bucks to be the same as creating authentic, healthy wealth in your life.

Creating authentic wealth, in all areas of your life, requires you to become a different person, and because of this, it doesn't make sense to assume that you will be exactly the same person when you achieve wealth as you are now. You will have developed better boundaries that serve you in order to increase your income, run a successful business, and draw the people into your life you need who are really capable of supporting you.

If you want to create a high level of wealth that provides you meaning, you will learn to say yes to things that serve you, even when they make you a little uncomfortable. You will also learn to say no to things that don't serve your vision. As conscious entrepreneurs we tend to have unhealthy boundaries when it comes to giving because we get so much of our self-worth from giving to others. The result is we tend to give of ourselves inappropriately and almost to the point of exhaustion, which results in bitterness and overwhelm, and it's one of the major reasons why conscious entrepreneurs fail at such a massive rate. You simply can't maintain giving, and giving, and giving, without receiving what you need in return. It's emotionally exhausting and energetically unsustainable.

As you up level in your business and your life, you will learn that you need to manage your energy in a different way or you won't be able to maintain success and happiness. This will enable you to serve so many more people than you ever thought possible because you will be serving the right people who are really ready for your services, instead of making yourself a martyr.

You'll also have more money, which means you'll be able to give in other ways like giving to charity or helping out people you really feel aligned to help. How many more people would you be able to serve if you had the amount of money you dream about in your bank account? When we are broke, we can make a profound difference on a small scale, and I'm not devaluing that. When we are wealthy, we can make a profound difference in unimaginable ways on a global scale. Which do you want to choose for your life?

When we fear people will want to take something from us, it's usually because we've been hurt or treated unfairly by someone we trusted. As you grow your business, you will refine your sense of intuition around where you should put your trust and energy. Will you still get hurt? Will some people still try and test your boundaries? Will there be experiences that leave you with a bad taste in your mouth? Absolutely. But when you are successful and making great money, you will move through these experiences with grace, and you will be able to trust yourself to do just that.

How would things in your business and life shift if you set wealthy and healthy boundaries that supported you in your ultimate vision?

_____

_____

_____

_____

_____

_____

Old assumption: I'm irresponsible with money, so even if I made a lot of it, I'd just screw it up, mismanage it, and potentially be in an even worse position.

How true does this feel to you?

1 2 3 4 5 6 7 8 9 10

Where in your business is this showing up? How is this belief sabotaging your wealth creation ability?

_____

_____

_____

_____

_____

_____

_____

_____

_____

_____

_____

Wealth Alignment Principle: The journey to creating wealth supports me in becoming resourceful and creative with my money.

This was a huge one for me, because in my early twenties, I ended up accruing a massive amount of irresponsible debt, getting extremely behind in payments, and wrecking my credit rating for years to come. As I started to grow my business, and I went from making one or two thousand dollars a month to making over five thousand and eventually having consistent five figure months, this fear came roaring forward.

I can't trust myself with this money. I never hold onto money anyway. I'm going to create another mess in my life. If I invest money, I'll never be able to make it back. My story was that I was so irresponsible with money I couldn't trust myself to have it. This created a wild fluctuation in my income as I dealt with this belief about myself. I really had to work through, and heal, this story in order to create sustainable income month after month.

This belief will push wealth and money away from you. Or, if you do create it, you will sabotage your ability to keep creating money. It can also result in hoarding or the strong desire to hold onto money, which can prevent you from making needed investments in your business out of the fear that they won't pay off. The Wealth Alignment Principle here is to understand if you engage consciously with your journey of creating more money, attracting more ideal clients, and expanding your business in the way that is perfect for you, then you will gain the skill set necessary to be able to make creative and resourceful decisions with your money.

There are ups and downs, ebbs and flows, in business, and this Wealth Alignment Principle gives you permission to approach every change, every obstacle, and every challenge with a sense of expansiveness and trust in yourself and in the universe, rather than approaching them from a constricted state of awareness. This principle also makes a great affirmation because the fear that we won't be responsible is really a deep belief that we can't trust ourselves.

Consider all the times in your life when you have been faced with a challenging situation. My guess is that you've actually dealt with these situations pretty well considering the circumstances. We are so much more powerful than we give ourselves credit for, and this principle reminds us to affirm that power rather than turn our attention to all of the places we've perceived ourselves to have fallen short. If you have been irresponsible with money, like I was, it offers you invaluable lessons about what not to do moving forward.

What would shift in your business and your life if you truly believed that you were creative and resourceful when it came to making great money and managing that money?

_____

_____

_____

_____

_____

_____

_____

_____

_____

_____

_____

_____

Old assumption: I'll feel wealthy when I have (insert your magic number) in my bank account.

How true does this feel to you?

1 2 3 4 5 6 7 8 9 10

Where in your business is this showing up? How is this belief sabotaging your wealth creation ability?

_____

_____

_____

_____

_____

_____

_____

_____

_____

_____

_____

_____

_____

Wealth Alignment Principle: You are already wealthy, because wealth is not an external experience; it is a mental, spiritual, and emotional state.

Another way of stating this Wealth Alignment Principle is that the level of external wealth you experience is directly correlated to the level of inner wealth you cultivate. Perhaps the biggest paradox around wealth and money is the idea that you'll feel wealthy when you hit a certain number in the bank account. I offer a new point of view, which is that contained within each one of us is the potential to create as much wealth as we desire.

In order to achieve the external state of wealth, you must cultivate a sense of inner wealth and luxury. The more deeply you can feel a sense of inner wealth, and then take actions aligned with those wealthy feelings, the sooner you will see wealth building itself around you.

Turn your attention to the places where you already are wealthy in your life. Do you have a wealth of friends? Of support? Of loving family members? Do you have a beautiful roof over your head? Do you have your basic needs met? Where are you already succeeding? It's possible to be wealthy in some areas of your life and not others. The good news though is that if you can achieve, or already have achieved, wealth in even one small area, you can replicate it and achieve it in all others. The more you turn your attention to those places where you feel spiritually wealthy, the sooner more money can find its way to you.

When you take time to focus on feeling wealthy, even when your external circumstances may not reflect what you currently desire, the easier it is to make powerful and profitable decisions that will enable that wealth to actually come in. Most entrepreneurs do the exact opposite of this. They think they have to wait until they have achieved certain level of wealth before making the necessary decisions to grow their business or to create a higher level of success. What successful people understand is that you have to make the decision first, from a place of inner authentic wealth, and then find a way to create the necessary resources. Wealth is a state of inner resourcefulness. It is the understanding you have the ability, already present within you, to create the resources for everything you desire in your life.

Where have you been playing small by waiting for things to happen, instead of embracing that you could create what you want right now?

_____

_____

_____

_____

_____

_____

_____

_____

_____

_____

_____

_____

_____

How would your life and business be different if you spent time every day cultivating a sense of inner wealth?

_____

_____

_____

_____

_____

_____

_____

_____

_____

_____

_____

_____

Congratulations! You've just radically rewritten your wealth story. How does it feel? I'm guessing a little exciting, and a little bit overwhelming, when it comes to how you are actually going to integrate this into your business on a daily basis. Don't worry about it, as it will all become clearer as you move through the coming days and week. You'll probably experience a lot of shifts and transformations if you actually did the work, and that's a very good thing. I encourage you to not judge yourself as things come up, but allow yourself to feel what you're feeling, and continue taking action toward your goal.

Just writing the story isn't enough. It's now about making the commitment to live in alignment with these new stories. Read them regularly if you feel yourself slipping back into old patterns of thinking. Even though you can sense the potential in these new stories for your life and for your business, it can be scary to really transform into this new way of thinking. A lot of people will do this work, get the inspiration, and then slip back into old ways of thinking. If you want to succeed as an entrepreneur and achieve true wealth, you'll have to continue doing the work of embodying and living these new stories. Have faith in yourself. I know you can do it!

CHAPTER EIGHT

The Three Essential Investments of a Wildly Successful Business Venture

A business takes investment if it is to grow. I know this sounds a little bit basic, and yet I'm amazed by how many entrepreneurs I speak with who are either spending virtually nothing on growing their business, or are spending money on all of the wrong things. The other thing that I see a lot with entrepreneurs who want to make a difference, especially those that fall into the coaching or healing category, is they spend tons of money on becoming better at what they do, or on learning another modality, and then spend little to nothing on learning how to market, sell, or grow their business.

Sometimes, as conscious entrepreneurs, we get so wrapped up in saving the world, we forget to treat our businesses like businesses. Anything in your life you want to grow requires cultivation, time, energy, and yes, usually money. Your business is absolutely no different. In this Chapter, I'm going to share with you the three essential investments that you must make if you want to run a wildly successful business that also provides you an amazing lifestyle.

Wealth Alignment Principle: Building authentic wealth requires smart and consistent investment

Obviously money is the thing most of know we need to invest. When we think of investing money, we often think of the money we need to invest to actually create our products, money spent to build our team, or money for marketing and advertising expenses. Those are all critical, and you must make smart and targeted investments every single month that are going to grow your business and move you toward your vision. You probably already know several areas where you need to invest some money, but have been holding back.

There are tons of books, resources, and mentors who can help you know what you need to be investing in and when you need to be investing it. In this Chapter, I want to take you to a different place with regards to investment by showing you three places it is essential to invest if you want to build wealth and see your business grow rapidly. I've chosen to talk about these three areas because they are three places where conscious entrepreneurs, especially, are extremely likely to neglect making the necessary investments.

They also aren't all financial investments. I believe that as conscious entrepreneurs, we also need to invest in managing our energy, caretaking our time, cultivating healthy boundaries, and an array of other areas in order to be effective for our clients and to exude an energy that draws money and success to us. I've chosen to speak to you about the three essential, and often neglected, investments that are going to give you an unfair advantage in business and help you succeed.

These investments all work in connection with one another. I mention this because there may be one, or possibly even two, areas here that make you really uncomfortable, and you may be tempted to think that you can skip one or two and just do the one that makes you feel comfortable. Remember our Wealth Alignment Principle about being uncomfortable? Keep it in mind here because you're about to be challenged.

Conscious Entrepreneur Investment #1: Your Self-Care

The more successful you become, the more important it is to manage and be conscious of your energy. You have more demands on your time. You have more you need to accomplish. You may have a team of people that depend on you to lead them. There are more clients to deliver excellent service to, and who require great customer service. Not to mention, the millions of other daily things that pull at your time and require energy to handle.

Most of us also care about showing up to these experiences with grace and integrity. We don't want to lose our temper, be impatient, or blame others when minor or major problems erupt. That is what makes this Wealth Alignment Principle so important. It is also what makes this principle a little bit different, because it's not so much about taking action and pushing forward as it is about knowing when you need to take a step back to rejuvenate and revitalize yourself.

Wealth Alignment Principle: True wealth is a relaxed state that allows abundance to flow into your life.

We often don't think of self-care as an investment, we either think of it in a luxurious fashion, a guilty fashion, or an obligatory fashion. If you're someone who loves to take time off and be pampered, then you probably have a positive association with self-care. If you're someone who has a really difficult time doing things for yourself, and you're always putting others first, you probably feel very guilty when you think about taking time for yourself. If you love your work, or you've trained yourself to be a workaholic, then you probably view self-care as something that you have to schedule in, or as something that is going to force you to sacrifice getting more work done.

I fall into this last category. I used to view taking anytime off as taking me away from what I love, and that was because I was getting 99.9% of my self-esteem from my work. It wasn't until I pushed myself to the point of burnout, while supposedly doing what I "loved," that I really understood the critical importance of taking care of myself.

You'll notice our Wealth Alignment Principle here deals with being gentle and allowing wealth to flow into our lives. Money will come into your life much easier, and at much greater levels, when you are in a relaxed and open state. Of course this is the exact opposite of our natural impulse. When we feel we need more money, what's our automatic reaction? To push. To constrict. To freak-out. To start running around trying everything, whether or not it makes sense or is likely to get results. All of these responses actually shut-off the flow of clients and money in your business.

Think about it for a minute, what type of person do people want to purchase from? Someone who is constricted, up-tight, and pushy? Or someone who exudes relaxed confidence and stability? Our reaction in times of financial crisis is to close down and to go into our heads to try and find a solution. The wealthy reaction is to remain as open as possible, while staying grounded in our body. If you can continue to make wealthy decisions, even at moments of apparent financial constriction, you will quickly bring abundance back into your life.

There are so many ways you can take care of yourself that will allow you to refresh yourself so you can show-up ready to serve your clients, and the world, in deep and meaningful ways, from taking a lavish vacation and relaxing on the beach, to getting a massage, to simply enjoying a great cup of coffee at a local coffee shop. When you're building your business, it's really important to consider the things you like doing and to build time into your day for them. It doesn't matter what phase of business you're in, or how busy you think you are, self-care is not something that should be neglected or relegated to the backburner.

For me, one of the quickest ways for me to rejuvenate and improve my mood, especially on more difficult days, is to pop in my iPhone headphones, turn on some great music, and take our miniature schnauzer Lou for a walk. It only takes me 15-20 minutes, is great exercise for both of us, and leaves me feeling ready to take on the world again. Therefore, I build time for this activity into my schedule every single day. I would argue that by building this into my schedule, instead of forcing myself to sit at a computer for 15 more minutes each day, I actually accomplish much more work, because I'm less stressed and able to be fully present for the work I do need to get done on any given day.

If you're on the verge of burnout, or you feel a general sense of overwhelm hanging over you constantly like a dark cloud, it's probably because you've put everything and everyone before yourself. Running a business in this fashion has an expiration date. How long can you realistically continue to work like this? What would be different for you if instead of approaching your work from a place of obligatory task doing, you approached it from a place of refreshed joy?

As conscious entrepreneurs, we are sensitive beings who tend to notice things intuitively and absorb more energy than your average person, which makes self-care of paramount importance. If we don't take time to process what we're feeling, to move through our mental and emotional blockages, and to release the events of the day, not only will our income suffer, but we'll notice our energy is lower, we feel overwhelmed, and we work in a way where we're constantly starting and stopping.

Appropriate self-care also increases your income in very practical, and also in some ethereal, ways. Practically, it means you come to every sales conversation, meeting with a potential partner, or whatever marketing activity you happen to be participating in, with a sense of high-energy and confidence. Confidence makes people more likely to say yes to buying whatever it is you offer. It increases the likelihood that people will want to partner with you, and it generally makes you more attractive. It's easy to see how your income will easily increase when you show-up to situations and conversations with a sense of relaxed confidence versus stressed-out, urgent, and frustrated energy.

Confidence isn't the only way that self-care increases your income, sometimes just by pulling ourselves out of the tunnel-vision that is our work-day, we enable the universe to send increased abundance into our lives. I can't tell you how many times I've decided to turn off my computer, leave work behind for a few hours to go enjoy a nice lunch, and when I return, there are orders waiting in my inbox, or the exact right person, who happens to be my ideal client, reaches out to me.

Metaphysically speaking, sometimes when our energy is one of pushing-and-pulling, the right situations can't occur. It's only when we take a step back, and allow the energy to move, that the right things begin to flow more easily. Remember, the Wealth Alignment Principle here, which is that wealth flows easily from a relaxed state of abundance. The more you are able to achieve a state of mental and emotional openness, you validate the truth that the universe possesses an unlimited ability to more than take care of everything you need. This creates a constant flow of money, clients, wealth and general happiness into your life.

Important note about self-care: it can be used as an excuse just like anything else. There are times when you need to go create money, get a client, or take action, and if you are consistently avoiding doing that because you need to take care of yourself, you're not a bad person, but being in business for yourself might not be the best option. I had a client, who I ended up firing because every time I would give her something to work on that made her uncomfortable, she would say she couldn't do it because she had to take some time for herself. Give me a break! Give yourself what you need so you can show up fully in your business and take the action that is going to get you the results you want.

In order to develop a healthy and sustaining relationship to self-care, there is one additional Wealth Alignment Principle you must understand, and it deals with de-linking two things that have been associated for what seems like forever: time and money.

Wealth Alignment Principle: Authentic wealth is not

related to working more hours, it's related to delivering more value.

Traditionally we have had tons of cultural and familial messages designed to convince us that working more hours will contribute to more financial success, and in many chapters of history there was some truth in this belief. Technology and the information revolution have absolutely shattered the link between working more hours and making more money. It is now possible to do more, in less time, than ever before, while still making great money. Yet still we find ourselves trapped in the fallacious linking of time to money.

The wealthy way of thinking is to completely over-deliver when it comes to giving great value, which is not always related to your time. You may be able to write several super-useful blog posts that could be dripped out to your blog over the next month in a matter of hours. You may be able to pre-record valuable trainings for your clients, that you can use again and again, with only a minimal upfront investment of time. These are just a couple of examples of the many ways technology has enabled you to deliver fantastic service while still effectively leveraging your time.

Wealthy people understand if you want to create sustainable income, you must build your business in a way that is scalable and leveraged. Otherwise if you get sick, want to take a vacation, or some other unpredictable crisis emerges, your income will dramatically suffer. Most conscious entrepreneurs fail to do this. They trade their services or products for dollars, and sometimes even make great money, and the second they step away from their business for even a minute their income plummets.

It is possible to work less hours, while serving more people, making great money, and having a much bigger impact on the planet when you set your business up in a way that maximizes technology, and is built in such a way that can be scaled, and takes into account the fundamental fact that you will need time for self-care if you are to thrive in business.

What are three ways you will commit to taking better care of yourself?

1. _____

2. _____

3. _____

Conscious Entrepreneur Investment #2: Your Education

The second essential investment of the conscious entrepreneur deals with helping you get the knowledge and develop the necessary skill sets required to market effectively and efficiently, as well as run a business. None of us came into this world knowing how to sell, market or administrate a successful business. We just didn't. Still, we tell ourselves that because we really, really, *really* care, and because we are smart people that there's something wrong with us if we fail at business. Or we assume because we really want to succeed, it will be enough.

You have to train yourself to become good at running a business, just like you had to train yourself to become good at delivering your services or creating your products. If you've never taken a marketing class before, if you've never been in heart-centered sales (much different than traditional pushy-sales), and if you've never created a successful business before, what makes you think you will be able to do it without gaining knowledge about subjects that, up until this point, you've had no reason to know about?

Of everything I'm sharing with you in this book, for me personally, this was the biggest and most difficult thing I had to learn. It's also the one big area of regret that I have, because I know I left hundreds of thousands of dollars on the table by saying no to investing in my business education. There is simply no more important investment you can, or should, make in your business than investing in your personal education. I said no so many times to working with people, or taking online programs, or joining high-end mastermind groups that could have given me quantum leaps forward in my income, my success, and in my business. If I seem exceedingly passionate about this it's because I am. Here's the Wealth Alignment Principle that encapsulates the importance of this investment.

Wealth Alignment Principle: Usable, highly specialized knowledge is one of the most valuable things you can invest in because it appreciates over time.

You'll notice this principle focuses on usable and highly specialized knowledge as opposed to generalized knowledge. This is a very conscious choice, because we're not talking about going and getting a degree in business or signing up for a class on business at your community college. There's nothing wrong with this kind of knowledge or education, but it's much more usable, profitable, and immediate to get knowledge from someone who has done what you want to do, and that you can put into action in your business immediately.

Many things you invest in begin depreciating the minute you buy them. For instance, a car loses a tremendous amount of value the moment you drive it off the lot, and so it goes for most kinds of consumable investments. Specialized knowledge does the opposite, it continues to appreciate and increase in value year after year. Why? Because you become a wiser and emotionally richer person, which means that you have more and more experiences to combine with that knowledge. You also have opportunity after opportunity to use that knowledge, and to refine and tweak it until you get maximum results.

I also view this as one of the most powerful, and sustainable investments, you will make in your business for one simple reason: no one can ever take it away from you. Your house, your car, your money, your things can all be taken away in a heartbeat. You get sick. A family member gets sick. You have to deal with some unforeseen crisis. No one can take away your knowledge or your inner resourcefulness.

When you possess the knowledge of how to become successful, how to run a thriving business, and how to generate revenue on-demand, no one can take it away from you. The power in all of this? Even if you lose everything, when you courageously invest in highly specific, highly usable knowledge, you enshrine within yourself the ability to always get back anything you may have temporarily lost or had taken away.

Right Support, Wrong Support

I'm about to shatter a major myth of the business coaching industry: there are very specific types of support that you need at very specific times in your business. I see so many entrepreneurs losing out because they get great support at the wrong time in their business. I also see so many coaches trying to create "catch-all" programs with little regard to the individual business owners, their specific industries, or where they are at in their business journey.

I've spent a lot of time thinking about which type of support will serve you best depending on where you're at in your business, and I've talked to many other coaches and mentors about this particular subject. Based on this, I've put together some loose guidelines for which kind of support will best serve you depending on where you are at in your business. The reality of running a business day-to-day is often very different from how we imagine it to be. When you invest in the right type of education at the right moment, it doesn't' mean you never have challenges, but it means you are given resources and opportunities to move through those challenges much more quickly, and to achieve results faster.

While you can, and definitely should, hire people to help you market and grow your business, you cannot merely outsource all of your marketing efforts. I once had a client tell me that all she needed was $20,000 and she would hire a PR firm, be on Oprah, and all of her problems would be solved. When I inquired as to what Oprah might be interviewing her about, and patiently explained that many people with $20,000 and PR firms aren't on Oprah, the line went silent. She quit my program shortly after.

You need to have, at a minimum, a basic knowledge of sales and marketing, or how are you going to know if the marketing someone else does for you is effective? If you aren't clear on your messaging, your branding, and your customers, how are you going to communicate to a marketing firm what they should be marketing or how they should be presenting you? There's a huge risk you'll be taken advantage of by an opportunist who promises you the moon, if you don't have a clear understanding of what types of sales and marketing processes are right for your business. Not to mention, the damage someone can do to your business or your reputation.

One of the other lies that entrepreneurs slip into denial around, and choose to believe, is the lie that you can just invest once, or if you just had one major influx of capital that would solve all of your problems. It's not true. You must continually invest, consistently in many different areas from your personal life, to marketing, to education if you want to create a sustainable, profitable enterprise.

For some of you, what I'm about to say next might panic you bit. Don't worry, I promise I'll break it down and make it manageable. Investing in your education is something you are going to need to do for the entire lifetime of your business. The minute you stop investing in your education, in my view, you need to take a serious look at if you still want to be in the business you're currently in. It's literally that important to sustaining wealth and finding new ways to extract meaning from your business and your life.

This information should not be taken as the final word on what kind of support works. For example, high-end coaching with a mentor who has a track record of helping people create sustainable businesses, if you can create the resources for it, is a tremendous investment if you know you are serious about growing your business quickly. However, if you are still unsure if you really want to have a business, you may want to start by getting your feet wet before you invest in a high-level mentor. There are those of you that are going to want to move faster, and those of you that are going to want to follow this very closely. Listen to your intuition.

I put this information together because sometimes when we need help we either find ourselves paralyzed, or we just invest in the first type of support we see, which may or may not be what we really need to create success. This part of the book will help you make an informed decision about what kind of support is going to be best for you. Armed with this knowledge you will be able to make a very smart and savvy decision about what kind of support you need to create more wealth.

Annual Earnings: Less than $30,000

I'm going to guess almost everyone in this category has aspirations to raise their annual income considerably. If not, I would ask you what fear do you have around making more money? If you've been in this situation for a while now, this section is going to be critical for you, because it's time for you to create a new level of wealth, and getting great support is one tool to help you do that. If you are new to business, you may not be that concerned that you are making less than $30,000, and that's great, but this section provides you an opportunity to grow quickly, and avoid the trap of getting stuck.

This can be a very scary place to be in when you're in business because it can feel like you simply don't have the resources to be able to invest anything. Believe me, I have been here, and what I know is that often when you feel the most like you can't invest, it's often when you need to find a way the most. Both because you need to get creative and resourceful to succeed in business, and because there are often some basic marketing and sales skills you're lacking and simple tweaks that will help you recoup your investment quickly.

Entrepreneurs at this level often feel like "if only I had a big marketing budget" everything would be OK. That's a lie. Do you know how to spend those marketing dollars? Do you have systems in place to measure your return on investment? Do you know what type of marketing copy converts leads into customers? Instead you need to focus on learning some fundamental marketing and sales skills, as well as getting deeply in tune with your particular customers' needs and wants. There is no way to outsource your marketing, for most conscious entrepreneurs at this stage in the game. Your goal at this phase of business is to figure out what your customers need, what they respond to, and how to most effectively market to them.

Individualized one-on-one coaching with an entrepreneur who has succeeded in business, is going to be your fastest and quickest route to getting these skills, but for many of you this may not be an option, either because of the price tag or because you're so new to business that there are a priori skills and systems you need to get in place. Here's a hint: in most cases, the cheapest business coach is not the one you want to look for! I'll talk more about how to find a great mentor or coach in the next section.

The important thing at this level of business is to get your feet wet, while still getting some really solid advice about what is going to work for you to build your business. That's why I recommend three things to get you this information, help you make cash quickly, and begin to grow your business. I am going to talk a little bit about the programs we offer because I want to give you a very specific sense of what this support should look like, so when you go to look for the program that is right for you, you have a clear understanding of what you need, and what you should look for.

1. **Basic Self-Study Courses on Sales and Marketing.** Our version of this is called Conscious Pathway to Success and we show you the basics of how to find your customers, how

to package your programs, and how to map-out a sales and marketing plan that will get you results. There are many other options out there, and what you want to look for are programs that will help you create a client-getting plan, while refining and developing your marketing strategy. Another great site to check out is Udemy, but there are tons of courses on here, so you really want to be discerning. Your investment level for these programs will range from $27 to around $997 in most cases depending on the program.

2. **Six-month or yearlong group coaching programs.** Self-study courses are great, but they often lack a community or accountability element that can be so important when you're trying to grow a business. Being around people who want you to succeed, are dealing with similar challenges to you, and who actually celebrate and support you is hugely beneficial.

Avoid programs that are purely mastermind based at this level, because you still need some concrete training. The best programs will have a self-study element where you can login and get great materials on sales and marketing, combined with some type of group coaching element. Also avoid programs that over-promise or are over-priced, you should be able to get the information you need at this level for a reasonable investment.

We actually provide two levels of support that are similar to this, known as our Wealth Creation Institute and our Wealth Creation Institute Masters Program depending on the level of business that someone is at. If you don't resonate with me or those programs just hit up <u>support@michaelmapes.org</u> and we'll give you our thoughts on a program that might be suited for you. Your investment level of these programs will range from $1997 - $9,997 in most cases depending on the length of time and what is included.

3. **Quality business building books.** Supplement this knowledge with quality books around sales and marketing like you're doing now. I highly recommend *Book Yourself Solid* by Michael Port. Books alone are not enough because they don't provide accountability, but they are a great supplement to being involved in a program and joining a community.

The most important thing is to pick a few tactics you learn from these three different kinds of support and actually implement them. If you can't enroll clients or create any income, it may be time to look at if there's a deeper emotional blockage you need to deal with, or if potentially being an entrepreneur at this moment isn't right for you. I don't say that to be harsh, but a business has revenue coming in and expenses going out, and you should be able to generate some revenue and clients if you engage actively with these kinds of support.

Annual Earnings: $30,000 - $100,000

If you're in this category, congratulations, you're no longer just playing office! You have a real, substantial business. I know for me when I hit $50,000 a year it changed everything. People stopped asking me when I was going to get a job, my friends and family took me more seriously, and I had much more confidence in what I was doing.

I realize there is a big difference between generating $30,000 of revenue a year and generating a six figure income, but I really believe that kind of support you need here is generally the same. Here's why: once you've figured out that you can actually make money with your business, it means that you have a viable and interesting idea. It also means that you've begun to establish your business and build a platform, which means that people are starting to take notice of what you're doing.

Because you've built your business to this level, there are a series of strategies you want to now implement to be able to double or triple your income. These strategies deal with raising your prices, beginning to leverage your time, continuing to expand your platform, and starting to market your expertise in a slightly different way. You're also reaching a level where you're going to need some more customized advice based on your business, your goals, and your particular industry.

Here is where I really recommend hiring a one-to-one business mentor or coach who can teach you these strategies, and also give you the customizable advice that you are going need. There are many great mentors and coaches out there, who really know their stuff, when it comes to helping you market your business in a way that feels great to you, and will give you really helpful business building advice. There are also a tremendous amount of armchair experts out there, who consider themselves qualified to dispense business information when they clearly are not.

There are many important things to look for when you're interviewing business coaches or exploring who might be the right mentor for you. The first thing I look at is have they done what I want to do? When I hired my first mentor, she already had a six figure business, and I passionately wanted to create a six figure business, so it was a great fit. In business there is a big difference between the theory of business and what actually works at the moment. A massive amount of entrepreneurs fail, and you want to make sure that you aren't learning from someone who isn't succeeding themselves.

Secondly, when hiring a coach, you need to look at their number one focus. In my view, profit and revenue should be the first thing any good coach helps you create if you are at this level of business. This is so critical because in order to go from $30-$50,000 to over $100,000 there are additional investments you are going to need to make, and consistent cash flow is one of the biggest obstacles at this stage of business. That is why helping you create more revenue, and a sustainable flow of clients, is essential to allowing you to continue to grow your business.

Unfortunately, there are a handful of coaches who don't really understand how to create revenue in any other business besides business coaching. Instead of helping you create profit and repeatable client-getting funnels, they will have you do a series of time consuming activities that take a long time to complete and have a very long-term return on investment.

Let me give you some examples of this. I spoke with a woman recently who had invested a crap ton of money in over a year of business coaching, and instead of focusing on increasing her revenue, she was being instructed to create a long eBook. I've also seen people with non-existent email lists, and who are very new in business, being told to implement advanced social media, email marketing, and webinar marketing tactics that make absolutely zero sense for where they are at in their business. Are you seeing the importance of hiring someone who can support you in doing the right things at the right moment in your business?

The third thing I look for is are they going to help me do business in a way that is in alignment with my values? For me, clients are not just numbers, they are not just people to pay me money, they are beautiful, autonomous individuals who have made a decision to engage with me and my company, and I take that very seriously. I also don't believe in selling people the wrong thing, or selling them things they don't need. I'm sure you have your own unique set of personal and business values. It's important to find a coach that will share those values.

Before working with me, one of my clients was working with a fairly well known business coaching company. It was a situation where you sign-up and then you are assigned to a particular coach. Let me say, I've also seen many situations where this model can work out fabulously; however, in this case, she was assigned to a coach who, week after week, just told her that she needed to cold call more people. This woman was the sweetest, most gentle person, and cold calling was a horrible strategy for her. Predictably, she didn't get results and was left feeling like a failure, when a few minor tweaks to her strategy could have made all the difference. She was paired with a coach who had a very traditional, and frankly, old school way of viewing business that was all about dominating others and taking super-unpleasant action. If she had found someone who shared her values she would have had a completely different experience.

The majority of business coaches do great work, and the best piece of advice I can give you is to be discerning and really pay attention to your intuition as you're choosing to work with a mentor. There may be times when you work with more than one mentor as well. For long spans of time in growing my business, I've worked with a private business coach, a private spiritual coach, and participated in multiple online programs at the same time. You don't need to go that extreme, and there are moments when I've went overboard, but I have always been glad when I had more than enough support compared to not having enough.

This isn't an ad for business coaching. It is an ad for what actually works. The bottom line is: when you're growing your business in this phase, there are many emotional and practical obstacles that you will face, and I firmly believe when you have a mentor in place, you can move through these obstacles much more quickly. There is also no substitute for having someone in your corner, who week after week holds you accountable, challenges your limiting beliefs, and is able to help you move through your energetic obstacles. A huge number of entrepreneurs never cross the six-figure mark in their business because they don't get the support they need or they make mistakes that are easily avoidable. Don't be one of them.

Annual Earnings: $100,000+

Perhaps you've already crossed the six-figure mark in your business. What a huge accomplishment! At this level, you probably want to continue to increase your income. You're also beginning to think more and more about the impact you want to make, the legacy you want to leave, and you're beginning to notice that even though you don't have the same financial fears, there are still important internal shifts that are necessary for you to get the most meaning and happiness out of your life.

If you're right around the $100,000 mark, you may also be working in a way that is very tenuous and still incredibly tied to your one-on-one time. It's critical if you want to keep growing, while being able to sustain what you've already done, that you begin to leverage your time and consider the scalability of your business. Can you deliver services, make decisions in your business, and can the business run effectively even when you aren't available to handle things?

Just as in going from $50,000 to over six-figures requires a specific set of strategies and things you must implement, the same is true here. At this level, there are three levels of support that I see as essential to catapulting you to continued levels of success and wealth.

1. **Individualized Attention.** You're going to want to have some individualized attention from a coach or mentor, or possibly even multiple coaches or mentors, at this level. The difference is you may meet with this person, or persons, less often than you have in the past. Coaching may take the form of meeting just a couple times a month, or even the form of quarterly or bi-yearly strategic planning days with a mentor or business expert. You have a lot more daily things to attend to at this level, and a lot more opportunities coming at you all the time, and so something like weekly coaching is probably less viable. You just don't need a coach or mentor as much at this level in terms of time, but you do need them in another way, which is to help you strategically plan the direction of your business.

2. **High-level mastermind group.** When you achieve this level of success many of your relationships in your life begin to shift. The people who used to support you often don't have the skills or resources to be able to support you in the way you need. I noticed a dramatic shift in my friendships and relationships when I reached this level of success, and it created a space for a new group of friends, colleagues, and supporters to come into my life.

This is why I strongly advise you seek out a high-level mastermind group of people at, or above, your level. You do not want to seek out people who are less successful than you because they won't be able to help you grow, and because you'll end up coaching them, and becoming disappointed when it doesn't feel energetically balanced. Masterminding at this level is important to figure out what is strategically working in marketing and sales, but it also provides a powerful container for you to gain more confidence, work through emotional resistances, and be lovingly challenged by people who only have your best interest in mind.

Many high-end one-on-one coaching programs with a business coach or a mentor will also include a mastermind experience. My high-end clients meet monthly for a mastermind call, and I know many other qualified business experts who have adopted a similar structure because they also see its transformational potential. Even though you are the most busy you have probably ever been at this level, successful entrepreneurs make the time to get the support they need, because they see its potential to move them forward personally and profitably.

3. **Specific education hacks.** This is what many entrepreneurs try to do when they are under the $50,000 mark in their business, and in most cases I think it's the wrong choice. By specific education hacks, I'm talking about getting education or training in very particular types of marketing that will boost your income, expand your reach, or allow you to automate more processes in your business.

Think Facebook ads, automated webinar strategy, email or CRM automation, or video marketing. Marketing strategies that should be implemented for a reason, at a particular time in your business, when you have certain things in place to be able to maximize the results you will get from them.

If you focus on these too early, you probably don't have what you need in place, or the money, to be able to really get the best results from them. That's why in the beginning, you want to focus on getting some general training around business building, marketing, and sales, instead of focusing on very specific strategies that might not even be right for your business.

When you are over the six-figure mark in your business though, this is exactly the kind of thing you want to focus on because it allows you to leverage your time, which contributes to continued business growth even when you aren't directly available. Either learning these strategies yourself, having someone on your team learn them, or potentially outsourcing them entirely, will help you more quickly create authentic wealth.

These hacks can take the form of online trainings, bringing in individual consultants, or attending live events or weekend masterminds designed to teach you one specific tactic or strategy. Coupling individualized support, with high-level masterminds, and education hacks, is a potent combination that not only grants you the marketing knowledge you need, it also gives you the container you need to continually grow emotionally and personally, which is essential to sustainable wealth.

Conscious Entrepreneur Investment #3: Personal Growth & Development

The final conscious entrepreneur investment I'm going to talk about is investing in your personal growth and development. If you want to create a higher level of wealth in your business and life, then the person you are needs to become a wealthier person. I'm sure that for almost all of you reading this book, you know you have some emotional, mental, or spiritual blocks when it comes to creating more wealth. In fact, if you've been doing the exercises up to this point, you're probably crystal clear on exactly what those inner resistances to wealth are and how they are showing up in your life.

Wealth Alignment Principle: If you want to create more wealth in your business and your life, the person you are needs to become a wealthier person.

Creating authentic wealth, as opposed to just making money, is about cultivating a sense of balance in all areas or your life, and realizing that if you're poor in one area of your life it has a ripple effect through all of the other areas. If you are stuck in your marriage, angry about your weight, or depressed about the state of your family relationships, it is having an impact on your ability to enjoy life and create more wealth in your business. The conscious entrepreneur understands the links between one area, and all other areas of their lives, and makes a commitment to become wealthy in all areas.

We learn so much about ourselves through being on this journey of building profitable businesses. When you commit to doing something most people never commit to, living life on your own terms, doing what you love, making great money, and not compromising your values, tons of emotions rush to the surface that want to sabotage your ability to actually create a life that reflects those things. That is why lots of people set the intention to change things, but never really experience transformation, because the shadow comes rushing forward and it stops them.

We often perceive these emotions as negative, which is unfortunate, because they aren't coming forward to punish us. They are presenting themselves to give us an opportunity to look at why a particular situation or event is triggering us, or provoking a strong emotional reaction, and giving us a chance to finally heal a deep wound or pain that has been there all along.

The idea that you are going to be able to heal these wounds all by yourself is fantasy. This is where investing in your personal development, whether it's joining a support group, investing in a life or spiritual coach, or committing to daily practices like meditation, affirmation or emotional freedom techniques, is of vital importance. Looking at how our personal wounds are showing up in relationship to our money, our wealth, or our businesses, is some of the hardest, most painful work we are asked to do as change agents. It is also some of the most rewarding, liberating, and ultimately profitable work you can do.

One of the questions that I ask my clients all the time is, "What do you get by not making six figures?" If you're already at six figures, then modify the question slightly, "What do you get by not making seven figures?" Because the truth is, if you weren't getting something from it, whether it's safety, not having to face your fears, or some other story concocted by your ego, you'd already have that which you truly desire. This question serves to clarify the personal resistance you have to creating more wealth. Would you like to answer this question for yourself now? Nervous? Do it anyway.

What do you get from not making six figures?

_____

_____

_____

_____

_____

_____

_____

_____

_____

_____

_____

_____

_____

_____

One of the best ways I know to move through personal resistance and into personal breakthrough is by listening to the voice of truth inside you. Most people refer to this as your intuition. My background is as an intuitive, and it's a huge skill set that I bring to the table for my clients, not only in using my own intuition, but in showing them how to harness their intuition to make quicker and better decisions. Listening to your inner voice will never steer you wrong. Unfortunately, most people don't really listen to their intuition, they listen to their fears, and to the part of themselves that validates their story and excuses, and then call that their intuition.

Your intuition will always give you a strong and confident answer. It will give you the answer you need, which may not necessarily be the answer you want to hear. It always come from a place of what is possible for you, never from a place of fear, and when you learn to deeply listen to it, it will always show you how to be creative instead of stagnant, in action instead of out of action. I'm going to share a small part of an exercise that I use to teach my clients how to harness their intuition to make good decisions and increase their income.

Take a few deep breaths, and relax into your body. Pay attention to how you are feeling, and release the need to make any judgments about how you're feeling or how you think you should feel. Continue to breathe in and out, and just step into a very present and relaxed state of being. When you feel ready, answer the following question. I want you to just write whatever comes to you. Sometimes you'll get a lot, and other times you'll only get a little, but whatever you write will be perfect for you at this time.

What do I most need to know right now, in this moment, to move my business forward?

_____

_____

_____

_____

_____

_____

_____

_____

_____

_____

_____

_____

_____

_____

Review your answer. When I do a much longer version of this exercise at my annual live event, Wealth Creation LIVE, I am continually amazed at the powerful information that comes through. You think I would be used to it, and yet it still astonishes me every time. Get in the habit of asking yourself this question regularly, "What do I most need to know right now, to transform this situation?" It gives you a focus, and a powerful course of action, and it is one of the most useful and practical ways to employ your intuition.

Of course, there are many other techniques that can help you heal and grow on a personal level that will enable you to step into becoming a wealthier person. It's an ongoing journey, and it requires an enormous amount of personal fortitude, to continue to engage with your own personal growth and development. You wouldn't be attracted to my work, this book, or me, if you didn't have that level of courage within you. Making the choice to invest in your personal growth and development doesn't only help you become more profitable and wealthy, it helps you extract much more fulfillment and meaning from the wealth and experiences you create in your life.

Now You Know...So Now What?

We all have the potential to find a way to make these needed investments in our lives and in our businesses. That is the truth. Most entrepreneurs won't accept that because it's scary, requires work, and casts a mirror on the choices and decisions we've made. Accepting this truth also forces you to step out of victim mode and realize that you are responsible for what you've created in your life, both the good and the bad.

Maybe right now, you're thinking, "That's great, but I don't have the money do to any of this right now." Or, "I will do this when the time is right." Or some other excuse is surfacing about how I just don't understand your particular circumstances, and if I did, I would agree that you don't really need to make these investments. This is personal resistance because your ego is scared as hell of you getting what you really want. Why? Because if you go through this journey, you will realize how powerful, how profound, and how magnificent you really are, and your ego will lose its job as the star in your own personal soap opera.

I want you to notice this resistance, and then ask yourself, "What choices do I really need to make if I want to create success, wealth, and meaning in my life?" The next question, after you've identified these choices is, "How can I make this happen?" I choose to believe you can make anything you want happen. I choose to believe that the universe will give you opportunity after opportunity, resource after resource, to help you make these investments. The first step has to come from you though. It comes from making a decision that these investments will make a difference in your life and in your business, and that you are truly ready to live, embody, and experience that difference.

CHAPTER NINE

Your Wealthy Future

I t is my belief that marketing, business, and sales are currently undergoing a major evolution, being transformed from forces focused primarily on the psychological manipulation of consumers into forces that focus primarily on helping consumers make educated and informed choices. This is not to say that we don't have a long road ahead of us. Evolution is rarely easy, and it's always messy, but it tends to get it right. The good news is that when you choose to be an entrepreneur who makes conscious choices about the way you market, sell, and conduct business, you become a part of this evolutionary process and help it along.

It's also up to us, as consumers, to make educated decisions about with which companies we want to engage. If we are serious about living in a world full of ethical companies and businesses, then we can no longer look the other way when it comes to which companies we choose to engage and do business with. If we want our businesses to transform, then we must transform the way in which we relate to businesses, corporations, and entrepreneurial ventures. We facilitate this transformation by owning our power as consumers. Owning this power takes many forms including choosing to purchase goods and services, sometimes at an initial higher cost, from companies that share our values and choose to be good stewards of our world.

Owning our power to play a role in the evolution of business on the planet begins primarily with an acknowledgement that we even have this power. For too long, we have been complacent. Content to displace our individual power to make a difference, by choosing to believe that we are victims to the status quo. We have bought into the lies that the old, institutionalized interests are too entrenched, or that one person simply lacks the agency to affect change. I am a living testament to what is really possible when you ditch the excuses and start taking action, every day, toward your vision. The stories of other entrepreneurs I've shared with you throughout this book are also positive evidence of what can be accomplished when you implement a solid energetic and practical plan. It is my deepest wish that you join us.

In order for you to join us, you'll need to transform yourself into an emotionally, intellectually, and spiritually wealthy person. This requires staying focused on your big vision while taking the small actions every day that contribute to your vision. In putting yourself out there, talking to potential clients, and starting to bring in some revenue in your business you'll become a much stronger entrepreneur, and a much stronger person. You'll notice you have to overcome your fears, take yourself more seriously, and find creative ways to avoid distractions and stay motivated. You'll also notice that other people start to perceive you differently, and more and more opportunities begin to present themselves to you.

This book is your guide, your reference book, your source for inspiration, but whether or not you actually implement the information contained within, will determine whether you alter your reality to reflect a wealthier existence. There will be times when it becomes incredibly difficult to continue moving forward and to keep the energy flowing in your business. During those times, I challenge you to ask yourself, "Do I really want to help people?", because if you truly want to help people, make a difference, and live your vision, then you will always find a way to take the action. If you're okay with not helping people, not having your vision, and staying where you are, then you won't. Choose to be a person who is in alignment with *actually* wanting to help people, as opposed to being a person who merely has a desire to help people.

I choose to see each conscious entrepreneur as one voice in a global chorus. We each have a note to hit and a chord to complete; unfortunately, too many of us have kept our voice silent or quieted for too long. When we choose to be silent, to remove our voices, we all pay a price. Individually we fail to experience the joy and happiness that was promised to us by virtue of our humanity. The people who desperately need our programs, products, and services fail to get the help they need to improve their circumstances; and globally we fail to avert the disastrous collision course we are on.

Alternately, when we choose to fully live and embody our purpose by exercising a wealthy way of thinking and taking action each day, we enable ourselves, our clients, and the world, to shift in extraordinary, seemingly impossible ways. Whether or not we raise our voices and lend them to the global chorus of transformation will determine whether conscious entrepreneurs create a song that changes the world, or whether we are forgotten as overly idealistic noise.

Choose to live your purpose. Choose to grow your business. Choose to serve those people you came here to serve. Choose to be conscious. Choose to be wealthy. Choose it every day when you wake up, and every night before you drift off to sleep. Choose it in the joyful moments, and choose it in the most excruciatingly painful moments. It is in making these choices that you will come to understand how much you're really worth, and how much you really deserve. When we are able to fully grasp that understanding, the understanding of our true value, we will finally know what it means to be wealthy.

ABOUT THE AUTHOR

Michael is an intuitive business mentor who helps conscious entrepreneurs make more money, get more clients, help more people, and step into their role as visionary leaders.

His unique intuitive approach to coaching enables you to quickly overcome obstacles that keep you from attracting ideal clients, and owning a thriving monetized business.

Michael's philosophy is simple: using the practical power of intuition, anyone can massively grow their business, reach their ideal audience, and make a big impact on the world. Learn more about Michael at michaelmapes.org.

www.ingramcontent.com/pod-product-compliance
Lightning Source LLC
Chambersburg PA
CBHW051901170526
45168CB00001B/197